Chiselled from Ash

LEN GAYNOR

WITH SHANE BROPHY

www.**HERO**BOOKS.digital

HEROBOOKS

PUBLISHED BY HERO BOOKS
1 WOODVILLE GREEN
LUCAN
CO. DUBLIN
IRELAND

Hero Books is an imprint of Umbrella Publishing
First Published 2020
Copyright © Len Gaynor and Shane Brophy 2020
All rights reserved

ISBN 9781910827208

Cover design and formatting: jessica@viitaladesign.com
Ebook formatting: www.ebooklaunch.com
Photographs: Inpho and the Gaynor family collection

Dedication

To Patrick.
Born sleeping, sadly we never got to know you.

Contents

« ACKNOWLEDGEMENTS »

TO MY PARENTS, Michael and Eileen Gaynor, for their early guidance. My father's urgings to keep my head up and shoulders straight, and my mother's great cooking – with cod liver oil and the odd tonic thrown in – set me up for the rigours of hurling.

To my brothers and sisters, who sharpened my competitive edge but never let me get ahead of myself. They backed me to the hilt always.

To my wife, Eileen, married for 52 years so far – you were always there to fill the breach when I was hurling; always giving me your full support while at the same time raising seven lovely children to complete our family.

To our family of four girls and three boys. I can only marvel at your progress through life and thank you for your kindness now in our twilight years. I want to acknowledge your wives and husbands as well – they have added so much to the cohesion of our family.

To our 18 grandchildren. It is a joy to watch your different personalities blossom each day. As you grow and your inquisitive minds open to the beauty of life, may you always feel the support and love of those around you.

I want to acknowledge all those who helped me in my hurling life. My club, Kilruane MacDonaghs provided me with the opportunities to play the game. The people who picked teams and got us to venues and guided us in how to play the game – they were starting us out on a way of life that would keep on giving.

I played juvenile, minor, under-21, junior, intermediate and senior for the club.

The last medal I won was junior 'A' at the age of 42 and I got as much satisfaction from winning that as I did from an All-Ireland. I want to thank all my teammates for giving their best on the field of play. I also want to thank all those people who run the club and continue to provide the facilities for our young people to prosper.

My secondary education in St Flannan's College, Ennis, where I received a very rounded education, was a happy time for me. To this day I have some very inspirational memories that were formed there. Of course, hurling every evening helped to erase the longing for home. Eventually I played Dean Ryan Cup and Harty Cup, winning a Dean Ryan in 1961. I left St Flannan's with a Leaving Cert, and a wealth of hurling experience. I am very grateful.

To play hurling for Tipperary was an honour and a challenge.

Tipperary people love hurling and love to see their team perform well - all is well in the world when that happens. I want to acknowledge all my teammates on those teams – minor, under-21 and senior.

Great men who gave their best for the blue and gold.

I also salute my opponents. I think the game of hurling suits the Irish character – a bit wild, coming from deep in the soul, it unleashes the bravery and dash that are necessary to produce the blinding skills that supporters relish.

I admire the present-day hurlers; their skill levels are sublime as they carry on the great tradition. Long may it continue.

Just like any game of hurling, writing a book is a team effort. Liam Hayes approached me in the first instance to write my memoir. Shane Brophy, the author, spent many hours with me in my home and put in countless hours on his own. He interviewed many fine hurling people to contribute to my story too. Thank you all.

I hope you enjoy reading this book as much as I've enjoyed recalling such wonderful memories.

Len Gaynor
August 2020

◀◁◆▷▶

BEING A SPORTSWRITER, writing a book at some stage was always an ambition of mine, so a sincere thanks to Liam Hayes and Hero Books for entrusting me with the responsibility of capturing the story of such a hurling icon.

I hope I have done Len Gaynor justice.

Len helped pass many Thursday nights in late 2019 as he regaled his remarkable love of hurling, aided by having our chats in his sitting-room which is full of medals, trophies and hurling memorabilia to aid his excellent memory.

For a Lorrha man to tell a Kilruane clubman's story might appear sacrilege to some but there is always a great respect between both clubs, and no doubt Len's strong family links to my home parish helped too.

A special thank you to Len's wife, Eileen and the Gaynor family, who helped make me feel so at ease with such an important piece of work as I sought to build Len's remarkable life and times into this book.

To all of Len's teammates, players he managed and management colleagues who agreed to contribute to this book, thank you for your time. I might not have been able to meet many of you face-to-face due to the Covid-19 restrictions, but the phone calls didn't lessen the impact of what you had to say about Len.

To my journalistic colleagues who have been such a great support in bouncing ideas back and forth, particularly Damian Lawlor.

To Gilbert Williams of Kilruane MacDonaghs and local scribe, Liam Hogan, who were an excellent source of fact-checking with access to their copies of club and county GAA histories. And to all the team at the *Nenagh Guardian* who have been so loyal and supportive in my career to date.

To my family, my parents John and Maria, my brothers Niall and Michael and my sister, Muireann, thanks for being there over the years. I might not say it often, but your love and support has always meant everything to me.

And finally, to my special lady, Grace for your love, patience and support in enabling me to complete this book, despite a little upheaval to our plans in 2020. There'll be even happier days ahead!

Shane Brophy
August 2020

LETTER TO THE EDITOR
Nenagh Guardian
Saturday, February 17, 1973

PROFILE IN COURAGE

Tipperary folk are so accustomed to their hurling teams successes that while followers are sure to praise their great efforts of their players, and rightly so, on rare occasions such as last Sunday at the Gaelic Grounds, Limerick, an individual player will rise to the heights of greatness which can only be achieved by few.

Under stress, as we are, from administrational level and cold shouldered as we are by a lukewarm national newspaper coverage that would prefer to dent the greatness which is Tipperary hurling, it was indeed appropriate and timely that one player should show forth and demonstrate the grit, grim determination and grandeur of Tipperary hurling by lifting our doubtful hearts and giving us one of those great moments which make life for Tipperary followers, at times, ecstatic.

In this tremendously hard fought and exciting game, on conditions which were keenly testing, Tipperary are down one point and with time almost out, forced a 'seventy'. Now the scene was set and the test was there as Len Gaynor, who had only a few minutes earlier previously brought our team within one point of Limerick by pointing a 'seventy' from a similar position, was being asked to repeat that performance, but circumstances were different now.

As the ball was placed, one noted the grim faces of the Tipp mentors and followers, and witnessed the referee running out from the goal and he pointed to his watch, telling Len that he must score direct to equalise. One also noted the grim, hardened, bloodstained face of Len Gaynor as he bent over the ball, harassed by the opposition supporters, he lifted and struck.

The ball sailed on and on high and unerringly between the posts, the umpire's flag is raised and our joy is Limerick's despair.

This is Tipperary.

This is Tipperary's answer.

Thank you, Tipperary and thank you, Len.

Yours was surely a profile in courage that day.

Yours sincerely,
"TIPP SUPPORTER."

« PROLOGUE »

I DON'T KNOW why I became so enthused about hurling. I know it was the only game around, but I really became caught up in it as a youngster, at six or seven years of age. The game was infectious.

And the hurling field was a place of wonder for a young boy.

One day, at a time when we were threshing, and all the neighbours were down with us for the dinner, I remember being fully awakened to the game and what it meant to everyone I knew.

There was a photograph on the wall in the porch in our house.

It was just inside the front door. It was a photo of an old hurling team. I had paid no heed to it. Until that day, it was none of my business as a little boy.

It was always there!

Big men with hurleys… and a lot of them with moustaches and that.

However, what struck me was, when the men were coming in to get their dinner, they stopped and looked up at this photo.

Someone pointed at this fella.

Someone else pointed at another fella… and another.

'He was a great one!'

'Yer man was some man to take a free!'

'And a lineball!'

Listening to these men look at the photograph and talk about games and deeds, left me amazed. The same men who were standing and talking about an old game were starving for their dinner. And yet, they stopped in their tracks.

They were stopped by old faces.

Memories of old games still fresh in their heads.

I would have been pucking around a bit at this stage, but I wouldn't have understood it that much. But watching those men and listening to them certainly tweaked my interest in the game.

I then took further interest in that photograph too.

It showed the old Lahorna De Wets, as they were called. They were formed up the road from my home in Rapla.

A meeting was held in late 1900, in Ballinamurra, to form a new GAA club in the area. Everyone was starting up hurling teams at that time; you could start up any group, as there was no parish rule then.

At the meeting the name Lahorna De Wets was chosen in memory of the South African, General De Wet, who had given the British forces such a rough time in the Boer war. They weren't able to capture him, and that news came to Ireland through the newspapers. People were beginning to talk about this De Wet. People here were delighted with him and how he was handling the Brits.

The first chairman of De Wets was George O'Leary of Beechwood. The secretary was my grand-uncle, Michael Gaynor of Rapla, and the captain of the team was Jack Dwan of Kilruane. De Wets usually trained in a field owned by Michael Flannery, near George O'Leary's house.

In their first year in 1901 they won the first North Tipperary senior hurling championship. They were very famous at the time and lasted until 1927, but then they disappeared and eventually the hurling was regulated by the parish rule where you couldn't play outside your own parish.

And the Kilruane MacDonaghs club was born in 1935.

But it was that De Wets team that really fired my imagination. To be like those men, and to be thought of, and fondly remembered, by a bunch of hungry farmers!

« CHAPTER 1 »

It might have been Cricket

MY BIRTH AND childhood, and entry into an early life of hurling, was all very normal but it might not have been. I might never have become a hurler.

I might have been a cricketer.

Who knows, I might have fought with my Aussie mates to win The Ashes against the old enemy England. I might have been Australian. An Aussie cricketer, imagine that?

And left far away on the other side of the world to watch the amazing game of hurling, or probably only get to hear about it in small snippets. If that!

Hurling might never have been *my game*.

As it turned out, however, I was born January 2, 1944 in Rapla, Kilruane. There were eight of us in the family, four boys and four girls and I was the second youngest. I was the youngest boy and there was a younger girl born after me.

My father, Michael Gaynor was from Ballinaclough, near Nenagh. He was born in 1899 and was 90 when he passed away, and my mother died two years later in 1991. There's great longevity in our family.

However, as I've said, it could have been so much different for me if my father and mother had remained in Australia.

In 1916, when my father was 17 years of age, he was involved in the local IRA brigade along with his older brother, Séan, who was OC of that Brigade. Eventually they became fairly notorious and had to go on the run during the War of Independence. They might sneak back at night to help out on the farm, with the cows and whatever had to be done.

Then came the Civil War.

Séan Gaynor inherited the farm, which was the normal thing as he was the oldest brother. My father got some money, but he had nothing else, so he had no choice but to emigrate to Australia in 1924 to look for work.

He left here without a trade to his name. He had to do manual work, and that was scarce at that time out there. He often said he was standing on the corner on a Monday morning and there'd be a group of men standing there, and a fellow would come along on a lorry and he'd pick some men – and if you were picked you were lucky and if you weren't you went home and tried again the next day.

He got going eventually. He was a good worker in different jobs, working on building sites and that kind of thing. I remember him telling me one time that he went in for an interview for a job and this big German man was interviewing him.

'Well, what can you do?' the man asked my father.

'I can do anything,' my father replied, so anxious was he to get the job.

'Get out!' the man told him. 'We have too many men like you.'

He moved on to where a new brewery was being built and he put in for work in it. He got in with the guys making barrels; he was an assistant to the coopers.

Anyway, there was a bit of a union in the factory and there was a vacancy on it. There were two men up for it and one would have been pro-management and one would have been pro-worker.

The shop steward advised my father that he should vote for the pro-management man. 'I won't,' my father told him.

'You'll either vote for him… or you are out of here!' came the second directive.

The coopers eventually heard this, that my father was going to be sacked because he was going to vote for the other man. The coopers called a meeting with management who would be fairly powerful, and they agreed with the coopers that he could vote for whoever he wanted.

My father was carried shoulder high around the factory floor.

WHEN HE WAS leaving the brewery several years later, when he was coming back to Ireland, they gave him a lovely presentation of a clock. And it is still in the home place in Rapla. He was actually promoted within a couple of years; he was going to be a cooper himself, so it turned out well for him.

He was in Australia for 15 years, and eventually he got married to an Australian girl called Eileen Murphy. Her parents were from Ireland; one was from Cork and one was from Limerick.

They were going grand and had their own house, and they had five children over there, Mary, Ned, Julia, Kevin and Des.

Three more were born in Ireland.

Maelisa was first.

I was second, and then Imelda.

One day, out of the blue while they were in Australia, my father got a letter from Ireland, from an uncle, asking would he come home and take over the farm?

There were three uncles at home in Rapla. They were all bachelors. One of them had died, and the other was about to pass away. The oldest man was then the boss.

He told his uncle that he would come home if Eileen agreed to come with him. Lucky for him, she did.

They decided to sell up the house in Australia and loaded all the furniture they could on to the ship. They were six weeks on the high seas, so it was a big undertaking with five kids; the smallest of them was only two years-old.

If that hadn't happened, I might have ended up playing footie in Australia.

Or cricket, more likely.

It was a big risk to come home to farm, but Irish farmers love the land and the lure was too strong for my father to resist. He was coming back to a good farm too with over 100 acres of land.

He wasn't home long when the Second World War started in 1939 and things became rough economically. The price of cattle fell through the floor.

It was a matter of trying to survive. On a farm you had a better chance of surviving if you had hens, turkeys, chickens and pigs so you were able to feed yourself. We also had around 10 or 12 cows.

THEY CAME BACK to an Ireland that was a far cry from what they had left behind in Australia. There was no electricity, there was no running water in Rapla at that time.

They just had a good house and that was it.

My mother came back to candlelight and had to start over again, learning how to work these things and cooking on an open hearth, which was very hard for her, but she never complained. I couldn't imagine myself, if I had to do with no electricity for a week, never mind a lifetime.

My father was okay about it, but my mother found it pretty hard, so into the middle of the 50s they built a new house. Electricity arrived as well. Water on tap! And, finally, a bathroom!

I always felt sorry for my mother and what she had to do. We never knew any of her sisters or brothers, and she had a good few of them. Occasionally, she'd get a letter in the post. Next thing she might start crying, having received word that one of them had died in Australia.

None of my mother's immediate family ever came to Ireland, and I never went to Australia. Some of the lads have been back there, but I never went.

I didn't have any interest in going, and I definitely won't go now.

The move back to Ireland was tough on my older brothers and sisters, too, particularly at school as everything was taught through Irish and they couldn't speak the language.

Mary was 11, and Ned was nine when they left Australia. They had started school over there and were well into it and well in with their pals.

SAVED FROM A life on the cricket crease, I became a hurler as soon as I could walk virtually.

They were all at it before I came around. They had no choice; in Tipperary it was hurling… hurling… hurling.

That's the way we grew up. We were rooted to the game, and the place.

Everyone we knew was rooted the same.

I became a hurler. I got stuck into the game and I just couldn't imagine life without it.

My father seemed to know a lot about hurling without being too interested but allowed me to do my own thing.

He was a wide-open character. If he got vexed, he would be cross alright. And he'd get uptight alright on big days, such as threshing day or something like that;

he'd get fierce excited.

But he was also the finest man, and a very good dad.

He never laid a hand on me.

I was on the Tipp minors in 1962, playing centrefield. We beat Limerick in the first round of the championship and were playing Cork in the Munster final and I was picked at centre-back.

We were milking the cows one day.

We had a milking machine at this stage.

'Are you playing centre-back on Sunday?' dad suddenly asked me.

'I am,' I replied.

'That's a very responsible position… isn't it? he continued.

'Yes,' I said, '… I suppose it is.'

That was the end of the conversation.

He did not need to say anything more; he'd made it known that he believed I'd be able for it.

My mother knew nothing about hurling, and initially had no interest in it. When I sort of got going, that changed a little. 'I am going to barrack for Len,' I'd hear her say.

Barrack was a word they used in Australia when supporting someone.

My mother was great. She was especially brilliant on nutrition. She wasn't thinking about hurling, it was more about health. She used to make a lovely drink out of rose hips, and we would be drinking it through the winter going in and out of the house.

All the time, she was building us up.

I had good strong bones. I got very few breaks and I would put it down to being well looked after. The big thing of course, which was wrong, was a big steak the day of a match. My mother thought that was great, and she believed it would stand to us but nowadays we all know that it stays too long in the stomach and is hard to digest.

Strangely, my mother started going to my matches, but my father stayed away; he never went to many. He simply stopped watching hurling matches; gave it up, if you like.

I believe he went to one famous match between Kilruane and Lorrha in Borrisokane, and what he saw wasn't too nice. He wasn't too pleased with myself and Des as we were causing a little trouble on the field, which we had to do, but dad simply didn't go any more.

He never saw me hurling with Tipperary.

One day, I was told when I was hurling, that my dad was sitting in the chair, listening to Michael O'Hehir on the wireless.

'Len Gaynor has the ball… and he's gone five yards…'

'Ten yards…'

My dad let a shout out of him.

'WILL YOU HIT THE BLOODY BALL!'

MY OLDEST SISTER, Mary, was 16 years-old when I was born. She went on to be a nurse eventually and worked in England all her life; married there and is still living there.

My next brother was Ned.

He went away to be an apprentice electrician at 16 years of age. He was a decent enough hurler but that move sort of finished him as he had to stay in Limerick, and he had no way of getting back home for matches other than on a bicycle. Limerick was a bit far away so he faded out of the hurling eventually. He won a juvenile championship with Kilruane MacDonaghs. Ned passed away in 2019.

The third in my family is Julia. She didn't hurl much really. She worked in Nenagh and spent all her married life in Ardcroney. Sadly, she recently passed.

Next was Kevin, who passed away in 2018.

He was just gone 80 and he was a lovely hurler. He played with St Flannan's College and played full-back on a Harty Cup winning team in 1954.

He joined the Gardaí and was a garda in Dublin all his life. He lived there and reared his family there.

Then came Des.

He was the farmer, and he still farms in the home place.

He was a good hurler as well, a hardy boy. The matches we'd have in the yard amongst ourselves would be fairly tough at times. I was a bit small and got knocked around a good bit, but they also protected me when they had to. I had to play in goals a lot.

They would be boring balls at me.

Maelisa then was the next sister and the first born in Ireland, and myself and herself would be very great. We used to get all the jobs, thinning turnips and thinning mangels. We were great at it with the hoes. The bigger lads would be off tramming hay.

She used to cook a few buns that morning and we'd bring them out to the headland, and we'd have them. It was lonesome work; the drills were very long, and it took a long time to get from one end to the other, but we always made it eventually.

The turnips were easy enough. They'd grow singularly, all you had to do was knock out a few and leave the good ones. The beet was terribly hard, though.

It grew in tangles, so it was hard to separate them down to one. It was very slow, very tedious. But we would knock good auld crack out of it all the same.

Maelisa and I remained strong with each other all our lives, since we grew up together as she was only two years older than me. She became a nurse in Dublin in the Mater Hospital. And more than once she gave me the benefit of her skills.

My youngest sister is Imelda, born six years after me. She also became a nurse in the Mater, but is now married and living in Lorrha.

I WOULD PRACTICE in the cobble yard at home, with a barn in front of me with a few holed windows and a barn door. I wouldn't just be hitting the ball against the wall; I'd be hitting it at an angle to bounce off another.

I remember that door still, and I remember my first real hurley.

We had all sorts of yokes, crooks we used to call them. You couldn't rise with it; you'd have to hit the ball along the ground. It was nearly all ground hurling at that time anyway.

But my brother, Des who was hurling with Kilruane MacDonaghs at the time, he went off to get a hurley for himself, made by a man called Philip Heenan, who was a great man with the horses. He had a great horse called Clover Hill; he was a great sire and great for showjumping.

Philip had hands that could do anything, and he made a hurley for Des using a spoke shave and a hatchet. He made one for me as well, a small little one and I remember Des coming in the gate on his bicycle with the two hurleys.

I stood there as he handed me the hurley.

It was like all my Christmases had come together. I'll never forget it. I was leathering the ball after that every minute I got. My father gave an odd growl if I hit a high one and it hit the slates on the barn.

'Mind those bloody slates!' I'd hear.

I learned to keep it low and keep it down.

I never knocked a slate off the roof, and they are still there to this day. But I rattled a few of them alright. I got hours of entertainment and hours of pleasure out of that.

I was a bit younger than my brothers and sisters; and they started going to pictures and going to dances, and I wouldn't be going so I'd be on my own.

Hurling was the way I filled in my time. It was a bit lonesome maybe, but I just couldn't get enough of it at that stage.

There was also a gable end on the dwelling house, a big high wall that had no window in it, so I was able to hit high balls and go in for the catch. Then I'd hit them higher again and catch them behind my head.

I would set myself targets.

I would try something new, a different skill.

I'd see how often I could repeat that same skill. Then another skill, something new again. Always counting. How long I could go without missing!

IN TERMS OF the farm, as I've said, I had the usual jobs for young lads around the place, pulping turnips and mangels to feed the cows.

Milking cows was great, however, and all the family had to join in with that. There weren't that many cows, still only 10 or 12 maybe, but still they had to be milked by hand and that was it.

One day we were threshing and were going to be working late and my father told me I was going to have to milk all the cows. It was a lot of milking by hand.

I started into them.

Some of them were very easy, very free; and some were really tough. Some of them would kick the daylights out of me, while more were grand and quiet.

I got them all done but my hands were shaking after it as my hands were weak. But days like that strengthened my hands, I know that for sure. It made them good and strong for holding the hurley and going into clashes.

I had that power in me.

To feed the cows, we'd also have to save the hay, which was a taxing job as well. The older men did most of the work. I did a small bit with the horses, mostly using a horse drawn scuffler to pull the weeds from the furrows between the turnips and beets.

WE ALSO HAD a lovely pony. She was a big, strong lady that was used for jobs around the yard. She also took us to Mass on Sundays with the trap and to Nenagh for shopping.

She was nervous and would bolt at the least thing.

For some reason she was never given a name.

One of my jobs was to take the corn to the mill for rolling. The mill was where the ABP meat factory is now located on the Borrisokane road outside of Nenagh town.

The mill was water-powered from the Nenagh river beside it. It made a loud low noise with the big stone rings crushing the corn.

The pony would be driven out of its mind from this, so I would have to jump off the cart while holding the reins with a very tight grip and make my way carefully up to her head, and hold her while the men took the bags of grain off the cart.

I then had to make my way to the cart and jump while still holding the reins with a tight grip. As soon as I would let go of the grip she was gone, like a shot. I could balance myself in the middle of the cart while she galloped for home. I didn't mind how fast she went then.

It was a great feeling. Mission accomplished.

All of it was really good hard work. Honest work, I suppose is the best way to term it.

And the type of work that makes any young lad a better hurler, and better prepared for whatever is thrown at him in a game.

ONCE, WHEN I was older, Des and I were doing a bit of reclamation on some of the land. There were ditches that needed to be removed.

There were an awful lot of stones, big rocks. We used a rigid plough and when it hit a stone it brought it up out of the ground. Nowadays with a spring-loaded plough, the stone stays down and the plough goes up.

However, we were trying to gather off the stones before sowing. The work took a couple of weeks and come the middle of March I was playing in the Railway Cup final on St Patrick's Day. I was murdered from digging the stones, some of which needed a big crowbar to get up, and then hauling them on to a big buck-rake on the tractor to lob them into the ditch.

When the ground was ploughed, our feet would be going down four or five inches into the clay, as we were lifting them stones up and out of it. The weather was cold as hell but, anyway we worked right up to the day before St Patrick's Day.

We went up to Dublin for the match and booked into a lovely hotel, and I had a lovely bed. I hopped into it and fell asleep.

They nearly had to wake me in time for the match. I was so tired, but I didn't realise it at the time; I had got used to the cold and working outside and I was hardened by it.

That St Patrick's Day came to be an awfully cold day, with sleet and snow, but I was flying it; it didn't knock a feather out of me. It was a lot easier than rolling stones off a field. I remember looking over at Eddie Keher and seeing him trying to warm himself.

It just shows that there is training in manual labour.

As a team, we had no training done at all at that time of the year. But I obviously had heavy work done and was strong and able for it.

The farming was always very good for my development as a hurler. Another day, I was turning hay with my father. We were working with two grain forks and it was just painfully slow, but it had to be done as hay was the only fodder we had for the winter.

I was arguing with him, anyway, as I wanted to go hurling.

'No!' he told me.

'We need to finish this field!'

I stayed with him.

I stuck it out. We finished what we had to do, and I was far too late for the hurling. But, you know, days like that probably made me a better hurler in the long run.

Len's parents, Michael Gaynor and Eileen Murphy were married in Melbourne on October 29, 1927; and Len (right) with his mother outside the family home.

The Gaynor family united in August 2018... Len, Ned, Kevin, Des, Julia, Mary, Maelisa and Imelda. Julia sadly passed in July 2020. She was predeceased by Kevin in October 2018, and Ned in October 2019.

« CHAPTER 2 »

An Education in Hurling

WHEN I WAS five years of age, I went to the nearby national school in Kilruane. It's not there anymore; it used to be beside the Catholic Church but a new one was built not far away.

I can't say I was interested in school. I preferred to be outside and preferably hurling. I didn't get on with the teacher. My name is Len Gaynor but in his mind Len, short for Leonard, was an English name. So, he asked me for my second name?

'James,' I answered.

'Seamus!' he replied.

Therefore, I was Seamus in school, and I was Len when I came home.

I didn't know who I was!

I COULDN'T UNDERSTAND it at the time, but the man was who he was.

He was very unpredictable; you didn't know when he was going to blow up. You'd be afraid of your life to get something wrong.

You can't learn that way.

We couldn't wait to get out at lunchtime and we'd hurl the living daylights out of each other. Once outside the door, there were about two or three yards of cobblestones and then we were out on the road. There was no field whatsoever.

We hurled away on the road, but it didn't matter as we still knocked great craic out of it. There'd only be one or two cars that would pass by and we'd have to stand in out of the way. Then we'd have to clean ourselves down before we'd go back into class.

They were hectic matches.

The road was rough and hard.

You'd wear a hurley away pretty quickly, but one of the boys got a smart idea where he got a shoe polish tin and he cut it and flattened it out, and attached it to the heel of his hurley. So, we all did that then, and the hurleys would last a bit longer. That was our simple but effective answer to wear and tear.

The teacher didn't like hurling; that was the other problem.

He'd give out to us if we came in sweating.

'You'll get pneumonia!' he'd say.

And he'd be shouting and roaring at us, so we'd have to wipe ourselves down before we'd come in after lunch.

But after I left school in Kilruane – I was only gone three years – we got into a North and county juvenile final in 1959 with Kilruane MacDonaghs and I was captain, and the teacher started to go to matches.

He made himself out to be a real true-blue Irish man.

IT WAS AT school where I played my first games of hurling, not competitive but they were good as they were between boys from local schools.

I was about 10 years of age when the sixth class boys in Kilruane organised a match against Ballinree school in Toomevara. The older boys picked the team and they said I was on the team for Sunday. That got me thinking…

God, I'll have to ask my parents can I go.

I didn't know where Ballinree was; it was off the beaten track a little bit, even though it was only a few miles away. But when I came home my parents said I could go.

We cycled up and met at the school.

It was only four or five miles or so away and we hurled away up there. I think they beat us, and we invited them back, and they came back the next Sunday. We played them in Beechwood, near Nenagh Golf Club and we beat them.

They were the first two matches I ever played even though they were organised by schoolboys, but they were well contested.

I wouldn't have been the leader of the pack, because I was younger. John Young was the boy who organised the school match and he did it quite well. He was waiting to be 14 before he'd leave school. He wasn't going to go any further.

If you were going to secondary school, you could leave primary school at 12 but he was putting in the time to reach 14 to get out of school altogether.

Also, in that group was Noel Peters, who was the same age as myself. I was born on January 2; Noel was born the day before Christmas, and that's why he was called Noel. Being born that late in the year meant he lost an extra year hurling underage. But Noel was a good hurler. He hurled juvenile with Kilruane MacDonaghs and then he went off to America and he was in the police force over there; and is still there.

We also had matches outside of school in the fields as well. The neighbours would come in, Michael Elebert, the Gleesons, the Slatterys, the Reddans and those lads. We didn't get as much out of that; we'd only get a certain amount as you'd only get to touch the ball every now and then.

However, I much preferred practicing on my own in the yard as the ball was coming back to me all the time. I got fierce satisfaction out of that and I really put my heart and soul into it. It was just the sheer delight of being able to do it.

The feeling of the hurley hitting off the ball.

The ball smacking off the wall.

Coming back to me.

And sometimes, it wouldn't come back right, and I'd have to just get around to it. I got great satisfaction in hitting the ball and catching it. I see it with young lads now, when I am coaching them, when they rise the ball for the first time and catch it.

The smile on their faces.

It's a big achievement.

People don't realise it is a big achievement. It's one of the first things they learn to do. I know they learn to walk and run, and they learn how to ride a bike, but to be able to manoeuvre a hurley and a ball is a big achievement and kids are doing it now at four or five years of age; and it is lovely to see.

I HAD GOOD footwork also which helped me move quickly and I'd put that down to trying to keep sheep from getting through gaps.

I used to look after the sheep fairly well. If there were any lame, I would bring them in to the yard and pare their feet myself, but to get them in to the yard was the problem. Getting them from one gap to another.

If you brought them to a gap, they'd stop and they'd look to go left and right, but I would be going left and right to try and get them through the gap, and I'd say it definitely made my ankles stronger.

Dancing helped too. I loved dancing.

I'd love to have done proper dancing lessons. I loved cycling as well which helped build up the legs when I was younger; going to matches in Borrisokane, which was about 10 miles away.

You'd get fit that way.

Everything helped.

To get around in those days, you needed a bicycle and I had one that was handed down through all my older brothers.

I was the last to have it, and it broke down under me eventually. Metal fatigue is what they called it!

However, it symbolised freedom, as when I had a bike I could get around. I wouldn't get too far walking. Cars only started to come shortly afterwards.

Between 10 and 14 years of age I was cycling to Borrisokane to matches. There were a lot of matches in Borrisokane at that time, good intermediate matches, and senior matches. We'd also go into Nenagh and see all the matches we could, but we wouldn't go to county matches.

It was rare enough to be going to see the county team until we got our first car in the early 50s; after that we started to go to matches in Thurles and Limerick. In Limerick, we'd go as far as Barrington's Hospital and walk the rest of the way, because we were afraid to go too far into the city.

It was agreed that we should always have the car turned, ready for home.

At those games, we'd watch out for a broken hurley, and if there was any length on it at all we'd be racing in to get it. There'd be fights over them, and lads wrestling to get the broken piece of wood.

The more I watched, the more I began to get a sense of who the best players were in the country. When we got the radio, we would listen to Michael O'Hehir's commentaries every Sunday.

It was in 1949, '50 and '51 that Tipperary won three All Irelands in-a-row. And then, through the 50s we'd be listening to matches on the radio and the minute the match was over we'd be out in the field.

We'd be Tony Reddin. We'd be John Doyle. We'd be Paddy Kenny. We'd all be taking different names.

That brought us into that era. I never thought I'd be on the Tipperary team. I was never looking to be on a Tipperary team. I never said I wanted to hurl for Tipperary; that feeling never came upon me as a young lad. I just wanted to hurl for any team that would have me.

When I got the chance to be on the team, however, I was ready.

I was made to be on it.

The pure love that I got out of hurling had me mentally and physically ready for the biggest step up of my life.

THEN THERE WAS KILRUANE MacDonaghs. Outside of school there weren't any competitions for juveniles until under-15 grade.

The club field is located in Cloughjordan, which is only eight miles from my house but I never set foot in the town until I was 12 years of age; the day I was Confirmed.

We used to hurl in different fields around the area.

There was a Mrs Gavin's field in Middlewalk. It was halfway to Cloughjordan and we'd hurl away happily there.

Then Johnny Moylan gave us a field.

There was Doheny's field in Ardcroney where the hurling and soccer pitch is now. They were just cattle fields, but it didn't matter to us.

We'd have bits of sticks stuck down for goalposts, or maybe a coat or a hat or something else.

When we went hurling in Ardcroney at the other end of the parish, the big thing then was to go into Ciss Heffernan's shop and get a pint of milk and a few buns afterwards. A pint of milk was a fair one at that time of the evening.

All the boys would come up and drink their pint of milk and have a few buns, and away home then on the bikes.

Tom Hensey would be there. Hughie Tooher, Tom and Charlie McLoughney. They'd all be there, hurling away.

Frank Diamond, Francie Ryan. All good men.

When I came up to my last year at juvenile (under-15), I was in St Flannan's College in Ennis. Lorrha had a good juvenile team before us and won the North titles in 1957 and '58, and we won in 1959 beating Lorrha in the first round and then Shannon Rovers in the semi-final.

We went on to win the North final against Toomevara, and then after beating Clonoulty/Rossmore in the county semi-final, it was on to the county final against the South champions, Ballybacon/Grange at Semple Stadium – my first time playing on the hallowed sod.

A chap by the name of Babs Keating was the star on that team.

Our management were smart and went to see Ballybacon/Grange in their semi-final against Moyne-Templetuohy. They said they had a good lad at centre-forward.

They said everyone called him Babs.

That raised eyebrows!

I was centre-forward on our team, but our selectors told me before the game that if we were not handling Babs then I'd be brought back to centre-back on him. I'd never played in the backs in my life.

I was always a forward.

By God, didn't Babs score 1-1 in a few minutes.

So, I was called back; and I wouldn't mind but I was after scoring a goal myself at the other end, but it was disallowed as the umpires said I was in the square; which I wasn't.

The report of the game in the *Nenagh Guardian* captured the beginning of our two careers; not that either of us had any idea we would become teammates in the blue and gold jersey for many years.

"Capt v Capt. Greek v Greek – it was a delightful encounter with Keating so often in possession but never knowing where Gaynor's hurley came from to dispossess him. Gaynor held him scoreless for the rest of the game."

Kilruane won 11-7 to 5-4.

At the age of 15, it was my first county title.

◂◂◆▸▸

MACKEY MCKENNA
(TIPPERARY SENIOR HURLER 1961–71)

The first time I saw Len Gaynor was in the county juvenile final in Semple Stadium around the age of 14 and who was he marking only Babs Keating. They were all talking about this Babs Keating with Ballybacon/Grange and he was the rising star. But Gaynor never gave him a puck of it when he went on to him. I said to myself that this fella will make it.

‹‹◆››

I WAS SENT as a boarder to St Flannan's, the beginning of my deep affection for that part of the country.

My father asked me one day, straight out.

'Do you want to go to St Flannan's… or do you want go to the Brothers (CBS) in Nenagh?'

'St Flannan's,' I told him, without hesitation.

It was as simple as that.

It was a considerable expense for my parents to send me there and it was for the education they wanted me to go there. They wouldn't have been thinking about hurling at all. Me? I wanted to go to Flannan's because I knew they had lots of hurling there. I had seen them hurling and had seen the pupils singing songs while the match was going on.

My brother, Kevin had gone there before me. He had won a Harty Cup medal and I got it into my head that I'd like to hurl with St Flannan's in the white and blue jersey as well.

I loved the hurling there, it kept us going.

The priests were very encouraging from the word go. Fr Jimmy Madden, who finished up in Borrisokane, was a pretty good coach when I started but he was sort of pulling out at that stage. Archdeacon John Hogan was there too. Fr Reuben Butler was from Dolla-Templederry; he was the man in charge in my last year. Fr John Shalloe from Clare too. They were always fierce keen into hurling.

I remember still the first day in class. It was mostly priests who were the teachers and this priest came in, and he happened to be Fr John Hogan.

'There'll be hurling training in the junior field this evening!' he announced.

I was thinking... *what does he mean by the junior field?*

My head had images of the junior hurlers at home, who would be smoking a fag at half-time and have different socks on them and all that. It didn't dawn on me that there were junior and senior teams in the school. I soon found out the juniors were in a smaller field. and the seniors would be in the bigger and better field.

There were no drills, no nothing at that time. We just picked two teams and hurled away.

I was delighted as that's all I wanted.

If you wanted to get a priest going and you didn't want to have too long in class, you'd ask him about some match. One of the priests made out that Jackie Power from Limerick was the best he ever saw. He rated him above Christy Ring, and I was surprised at that. But he was a good judge, this man.

We'd get him talking about hurling, and he'd talk about hurling all day long.

We hurled every evening after school for three-quarters of an hour. It was lovely because there was a great attitude towards hurling, and football as well. There were lads there from Clare, of course. A big number of lads used to go from North Tipperary to St Flannan's at that time. Donie Nealon was just gone, as he was the same age as my brother Kevin. Fr Seamus Gardiner was just gone as well and came back, just after I left, as a teacher. Willie Walsh came back as a teacher too, after I left. Later, he would become the Bishop of Killaloe and a selector with me with Clare.

There was Willie Moloney from Ballyphilip in Silvermines. We picked him up and took him to St Flannan's, as our fathers were friendly. I was friends with him all the time down there. There was a Bill Dwyer from Toomevara, we were close as well. Denis McLoughney from Ardcroney also came the next year.

There were lads there from as far away as Kerry; there was a great catchment area for hurlers in Flannan's at the time and, of course, as we were boarders, we had lots of time on our hands.

It was fairly intimidating starting off.

The college is a big campus in the centre of Ennis town, with a huge big building in the middle with all these classrooms and dormitories. It was easy enough to make friends though. We'd all be out on the field together. Every evening after school... rain or shine. Everyone was supposed to go out.

Some lads didn't want to, and I thought that was their choice. They had no interest in hurling or football.

But they were still told to get out and play!

They never had to tell me to go out.

I was out the door.

I couldn't get out quickly enough to hurl.

ON SUNDAYS, WE could have two matches.

If the senior team won a match, we'd get a day off. We'd play a match in the morning and go into our dinner in our togs and jerseys; and then go out and play another match in the afternoon.

We had money matches as well.

We were like professionals!

You paid six pence into a fund and one of the senior lads would collect it. It would be for the juniors only. The Harty Cup team wouldn't be involved in this, but it was open to anyone from second year to fourth year.

The money was pooled, and all the teams picked.

The big secret in picking a team was to know how good the first years were. No one would know really, but if you could find out if a first year was good and you had him on your team, it would be a bonus.

You could win a half crown or three shillings if you won the tournament.

I'll tell you how important a half crown was at that time. I got 10 shillings from my father when I was going to school for each term, and that had to last me from September to the Christmas holidays.

In Flannan's, we wouldn't be outside the gates of the school, unless there was a big match on. Money was very scarce but there was never much to spend it on either. They did open a shop when I was there, and it would be open only on a Sunday. It had ice cream and minerals. Whatever it was about us, we used to buy a big bottle of Cidona and an ice cream and mix them together.

Shake it, and then drink it.

It was called a fizz-bomb, and it was amazing.

The food wasn't great though. And what we got never filled us. For breakfast it was loaf bread, butter, and jam. There'd be wagons of tea, made in big kettles with milk and sugar; the whole lot thrown into it.

Then we'd get a slice of loaf bread with jam but no butter around 1 o'clock. In the afternoon, when school would be over at three or four o'clock, we'd get dinner. It might be a bit of beef some days, but it would be a very small portion. We'd be looking to borrow a bit from other lads. Parents might send in an odd cake, which we'd keep up in our room.

I was never homesick. I used to write home every week and they'd write a letter back to me. It was a different world really.

We just put up with it.

There was no... 'Can I come home?'

The answer would have been... 'No!'

And that was it; you stuck it out.

But it was okay. There was no bullying or anything like that, not in my experience. I lived for the hurling and only for that I wouldn't have been able to stay. The hurling kept me going and a lot of the schools matches at the time were played in Nenagh and I'd tip out home after for an hour, maybe.

FROM AN EARLY stage I was able to hold my own with everyone on the field. I didn't count myself great or expect to be on county teams or anything like that. But in my second last year I was on the Harty Cup team and there was another lad there from Tipperary who didn't make it.

I came home for the summer holidays, and the next thing I saw the Tipperary minor team in the papers, and the lad who couldn't make the team in Flannan's was chosen ahead of me.

I don't know how that came about, but I found out he was from a prominent club and they held sway that time. He was also a 'back man' and I was a 'back man' as well. Anyway, finally I made the Tipp minor team the following year when I was finished at Flannan's in 1962.

We had won the Dean Ryan in 1961; we beat De La Salle Waterford in the final and I was the captain. It was a big win for Flannan's as they hadn't won the cup for a few years.

I was on the Harty Cup team in '59 and I played with them for a couple of years, but we didn't win anything. If you were on the Harty Cup team, you got Bovril around 11am, which was extra to what everyone else got.

No one got Bovril, only the team.

We also got served up a raw egg.

And we ate it! Sure, we'd eat anything at that time.

The teachers wanted to win the Harty Cup all the time.

There was fierce pride in the Harty Cup. It was *the* competition.

Thurles CBS were very strong. St Colman's of Fermoy, North Monastery and Coláiste Chríost Rí from Cork were very strong also.

However, I hardly won a match in the Harty Cup in my three years on the team. We just weren't good enough. We hadn't enough good lads, though we had talent. Jim Woods, who hurled with Clare after, was on the team, as were Noel and Dickie Pyne also from Clare. They were there or thereabouts at county level, but they didn't really make it with the county at senior level.

There was Brendan Hennessy from Ballyduff in Kerry. When I went to St Flannan's first, he was in his last year when I was in my first year on the team and he was the star player. He was a great footballer and a great hurler. I played against him after for Tipperary in New York. He went to live in the States shortly after leaving Flannan's and he was on their team for a long number of years.

I met him out there but, one day a few years ago, didn't he land here at the door in Kilruane on a visit home from New York. He found out where I was living, and he came out and we had a great chat.

Clare great, Jimmy Smith would come in an odd time and give us a training session. I remember him taking 21-yard frees against us. I remember, especially, barely getting my head out of the way one time as the ball was coming straight for me.

On the Harty Cup team, they put me wing back whereas I would have been centre-back on the Dean Ryan team. We also played against the past pupils, which was a big thing at that time. Whether they heard I played in the backs in the county juvenile final I don't know, but the next day in training, I was told to go back to wing back.

I was put left wing back, and I hurled left-wing back for the rest of my life.

Tipp put me left wing back, everyone put me left wing back.

I don't know why. Maybe it was because I could hit the ball on both sides.

I loved wing back in the end.

It was a smashing position to play. You had to mark your man but at the same time you had a little freedom, providing cover for the centre-back and sweeping up the breaking ball.

It is a position that demands a lot of concentration and if you study the game properly you can nearly anticipate where the ball will land before it drops and be in the right position to clear the danger.

There are certain qualities you need for a half-back. First of all, you have to be very sharp. It's a key line as if the ball gets past you, the full-back line is vulnerable and there are only a few players left to defend the goal. I always stood behind my opponent when it came to defending but close enough to let him know I was there.

In my day, the primary role of a defender was to stop the opponent scoring, with a lesser focus on supplying quality ball to the forwards. That certainly has changed so a half-back has to be a quality hurler nowadays.

IN MY LAST year in St Flannan's I was captain of the Harty Cup team.

I actually captained three teams in that year; the senior team, junior team and the junior football team. All the junior matches were in the evening time, during study time and I thought my Leaving Cert would suffer as a result, but it didn't. I surprised myself.

We did seven subjects for the Leaving Cert, including Greek and Latin.

We were supposed to be learning from the great philosophers and those lads, on how they thought and all that sort of stuff. I just did my work in class. I wasn't brilliant or anything like that.

It was only the really good lads who went on to university. They used to bring in different professional people to talk to us about their work... solicitors, vets, and the like, which was good at the time. It was the early 60s, they were ahead of their time that way.

Despite the tradition of hurling, we still had to study.

We had study from five to seven o'clock in the evening.

We'd stop for supper, and study again from a quarter to eight to half nine. We had to fill in that time, we just couldn't get out. It was tough going that way because we'd be jaded by the time half nine came around.

All we were fit for was the bed.

The Kilruane MacDonaghs team that won the Tipperary juvenile championship in 1959. Back row (from left): William Sheppard, Jim Casey, Phil Gaffney, Séan McLoughney, Séan Gaffney, Tony Heffernan, Liam Heffernan, Denis McLoughney, Jim McLoughney. Front row (from left): Joe Brophy, Séan White, Séan Dwan, Len Gaynor (captain), Séan Ryan, Liam Daly, Liam Ryan. Seated: Connie Keogh and Pat Waters.

And (below) Len displays the silverware after the victory.

« CHAPTER 3 »

Making County

AFTER COMPLETING THE Leaving Cert in 1961, I came home to Kilruane before I got a job with the ESB in Limerick.

I was in the drawing office where they had all the drawings and maps of electrical lines around the Limerick area. I was there for a while, but I felt out of place. I didn't like being stuck in an office all day. At the same time it was grand, I got a bit of experience and I opened up a bit in terms of my personality.

I used to stay in digs in Limerick city and get home on a Friday evening and then get a lift back on the Monday morning. It was a bit awkward for the hurling.

I was still in Limerick when I got on the Tipperary senior panel in 1964. I was on the under-21 team at the time when I was called up to the senior panel and I went into training for the first time on the Friday night I was home.

Mackey McKenna was the furthest away that time in Borrisokane and whoever was the furthest away brought their car and filled it. You'd have Mick Burns in Nenagh, Donie Nealon in Newtown, Liam Devaney in Borrisoleigh, so we'd have a full load going into Thurles.

County secretary, Tommy Barrett came up to me after training one evening and he asked me, 'Where do you come from for training?'

I told him I'd be in Limerick on a Tuesday night.

'How are you going to get in from there,' he said.

'I don't know,' I replied.

'Have you a car?'

'I haven't,' I said, '… but I can drive!'

'Ah there's hardly any need for you to come in… you're fit enough,' he said.

That's where Jim Stapleton came in. He was a selector from Solohead, and he overheard the conversation and he said, 'That man has to be got in here… I don't care how you get him here.'

So, the upshot of it was that I had to hire a car in Limerick and drive to Thurles. They made me drive down around West Tipperary, through Cashel and pick up John O'Donoghue and Peter O'Sullivan and bring them to training, so I'd be earning my way with the car.

I WAS IN Limerick for a couple of years, but I was dying to get out of the ESB office. Then I heard about a job going with Dovea AI and I applied for it in 1964.

AI (Artificial Insemination) is as a way of impregnating cows without the need for a bull by taking semen from the bull and putting it into straws from where the likes of myself would be able to inseminate the cow as a bull would naturally do.

It was a relatively new process at the time, having been developed in the 50s but it was really becoming popular among farmers in the early 60s so they needed more staff. That was really the peak time; then it started to die off and nowadays most farmers are doing it themselves without the need for the AI man to call in.

I had to do an exam to join Dovea AI and passed it. Being a farmer's son certainly didn't do me any harm.

You had to be trained then how to do it. It suited me down to the ground. I was able to farm as well in the evenings. It was a job I stayed in for the next 38 years.

It was a little bit tough with the hurling because the busy time with AI would be in the spring and that would be the busy time for the hurling as well. It was tough going because you had to work Saturdays and Sundays. That was obligatory and it was hard enough to fit it in.

In 1966 we were playing Limerick in the first round of the Munster Championship in Cork and I decided to try and do my AI calls on Sunday morning. I was working around the Lorrha area and when I finished, I had a farmer organised to drive me straight away to Cork. I had my gear in the car ready to go.

We left Ardcroney around twelve o'clock and got to Cork around two o'clock, and the match was at three o'clock so there wasn't much time for rest or thinking about it. It was a little bit awkward, but I managed it. It would take its toll a bit, but it was better than sitting at home, not that I'd do too much of that anyway.

AI would take you at certain times outside my local area. I'd be going to farms in Offaly and Laois as well. I'd go into a place where there might be a bachelor on his own and the minute he'd hear my name, he'd be talking hurling straight away. It was just amazing. They could be the most remote places and they'd be smarter about hurling than I was.

In the 90s, I was well and truly finished hurling when I went into this farm that I was never in before. It was down a long lane, and when I got to the end of it and I pulled up, this man came out and he says… 'Len Gaynor?'

'That's right,' says I.

'You played your first match for Tipperary in 1962 as a minor below in Cork against Limerick.'

'Be God,' I said, 'You know your hurling.'

He looked proud of himself. 'When I go down to the pub on a Sunday night, there's no one can beat me at the hurling.'

AFTER HURLING JUVENILE for Kilruane up to 1959, I moved up to minor where we reached the North final, but we were well beaten by a fine Roscrea team in '61. I also was on the North Tipperary minor squad that took part in trials for the county team, but I didn't make it.

I also played for the club in the new under-21 grade in 1961, as well as making the intermediate team at wing back.

My first match was in Borrisokane against Knockshegowna and was that tough, I'm telling you. That was tough, really tough.

We didn't last too long in the championship; it was knockout, and we were eliminated fairly early on. I was very young for that, just 17. It was an education I can tell you; my eyes were opened. Frank Diamond was centre-back, I was wing back.

The funny thing about it was in the few games we did play, some players were being watched to become part of the Tipperary junior panel for the following year and I was called up for the first trial in Borrisokane and I said I'd go.

I wasn't picked to play but I was picked as a panellist. When I got there, half the lads hadn't turned up so I got to play, and I must have played well because I was picked for the next trial. I must have played well in that too, because I was picked again.

The final trial was in Nenagh and I played it and I remember having an awful collision with one big fella. I was still only 17 but I came out of it okay. It was a baptism of fire in adult hurling.

We all went for a cup of tea afterwards in the nearby Ormond Hotel. One of the selectors came over to me and said, 'You're on the panel.'

'Great,' I said.

The next thing I got word that I wasn't.

Tipperary County Board had decided that they wouldn't allow anyone that was eligible for minor to play with the junior team. So that finished that, but it led on to trials for the minor team.

TO BE HONEST, I wasn't really expecting a call up to the Tipperary minors in 1962. Some people would be saying, you should be on the team. One fella came up to me after that. He was on the senior panel and he said, 'They have recognised you at last!'

Getting on to the Tipperary team wouldn't have been on my radar, but I remember the day we won the Dean Ryan Cup final with St Flannan's. The referee was a man named Jim Stapleton who was a Tipperary selector. I didn't know him at the time. I remember him coming into the dressing-room afterwards.

'Where's Gaynor?' he asked aloud.

He wanted to get a look at me. I must have played well and caught his eye.

The boys gave a big cheer when they heard that; they thought I was going to make the grade.

That was the first inkling I had that I might make county. I had never any notions in my head that time about making a Tipperary team.

I got on the Tipp minors and I was hurling flat out from then on. Our first championship match was against Limerick in Cork, as my old farmer friend in Laois was able to recollect.

The Tipp seniors were playing Limerick the same day.

There was a man called Paddy Burke and he had a hackney car in Roscrea; he was the official driver for this area. He picked me up at home that Sunday morning.

We were all day going down. Paddy wouldn't pass 40 miles an hour despite having a fine big car. He liked to take his time. We eventually got there and won, beating Limerick fairly well.

I was centrefield that day. Babs Keating was also on the team; Noel O'Gorman, Francis Loughnane as well. We had a good team.

We played Cork in the Munster final and I was picked at centre-back and we beat them well and went on to the All-Ireland final against Kilkenny, who were going for three in-a-row.

Our final preceded the senior final where Tipperary would beat Wexford.

In the minor final, Kilkenny were ahead but we were coming back at them. I stepped up to take a '70' and landed it just over the crossbar on the roof of the net. A huge roar went up, as the Tipp crowd had started to come in during the second-half. That was the first time I experienced such cheering.

That score drew us level, but Tom Walsh got a ball after the puckout and scored a goal for Kilkenny and that finished us.

That was my first real experience of big match occasions. You'd be bumping into the Tipperary senior lads in Thurles at training and you'd see some of them passing in and out, admiring them.

It was a different world to the club scene with fellas from all over the county. You learn a bit from all those lads as well. I got on well with them all.

I was especially friendly with Babs.

1962 WAS MY only year at minor with Tipperary. I enjoyed it, as it was serious hurling at that level. You'd learn a lot from your opponents as well as your own lads at training. It was a step up.

I was never worried about playing a match, no matter who I was playing against or who the opposition was, it didn't bother me, I just wanted to play and beat whoever my opponent was. I never had any fear of anyone that way.

Back then, you wouldn't know much about an opponent anyway. Not like now.

With the club we progressed to a North senior final against Toomevara in Nenagh. My brother, Des played at midfield also, but we went down by two points.

However, we still progressed to the county quarter-final where we defeated Cappawhite, setting up a semi-final against a Thurles Sarsfields side who were proving to be a nemesis of Kilruane at the time. However, it was a Sarsfields side that contained the likes of Tony Wall, Séan McLoughlin and Jimmy Doyle, who won 10 county titles in 11 years.

IN 1963 THERE was nothing much going on at county level, but I was playing senior with Kilruane MacDonaghs in the North Tipperary League, which was established that year to go alongside the championship.

Toomevara were a big team at the time. Roscrea were very strong as well. Lorrha were strong too.

On the Kilruane team were the likes of Gerry McCarthy, who was a real stylist. Jimmy Gibson, Tom Hensey, Ger Hogan, Hughie Tooher. My own brother, Des would have been there for a good while. Séan Hyland was there too, along with Tom and Charlie McLoughney. They were all well known around North Tipperary, as some of them had played with Tipp. Tom McLoughney had played with Tipp a lot; Gerry McCarthy played a bit; Jimmy Gibson played in the league as well and won a league title.

It was a strong dressing-room. It was nice to get on that team. It was great to have those fellas around me, minding me if you like and encouraging me.

In the 1963 championship we were defeated by Roscrea in the first round which sent us into the losers group, where we defeated Moneygall and drew with Kiladangan in a tremendous game, before winning the replay three weeks later. Newport were the opponents in the losers group final which we won by a point to put us back in the championship proper, where we drew with Toomevara, but they won the replay and we were out finally.

I WAS CALLED into the Tipperary under-21 panel the following year, in 1964, in what was the first year of that championship at county level.

I received a letter in the post which told me to be in… *"Tipperary Town to play*

Cork in the first round of the Munster Championship on Sunday, May 31st".

Kilruane were playing Roscrea in Nenagh in the North championship the same day, which Roscrea won. Francis Loughnane and Owen Killoran from Roscrea were also playing. After being rivals for 60 minutes in a tough game for our clubs, the three of us hopped in a car straight after the match and off we went to play against Cork.

We were managed by Séan Ryan from West Tipperary. John Joe Maher was a selector from Roscrea as well as they had good minor teams at that time. Martin Loughnane would have been there too.

We beat Cork and then overcame Clare in the semi-final.

Waterford awaited in the Munster final. We ended up winning it comfortably, but it was another tough game.

Anytime I got the ball and hit it, my marker would chop down on my wrist and he did it three times. I ended up breaking my wrist. I didn't go off. I was okay until the Tuesday afternoon, when I couldn't bear the pain of it any longer. I went to the hospital and they said it was broken, and it was put in plaster.

The injury kept me out of the All-Ireland semi-final against Roscommon, but I was back for the final against Wexford in Nowlan Park, where I won my first All-Ireland medal.

Babs Keating was inspiring that day, as were Mick Roche and Joe Fogarty at midfield and Noel O'Gorman at full-back.

I was still underage when we reached the All-Ireland final again in 1965 but Wexford got their revenge with Tony Doran doing the damage, and not for the first time in my county career.

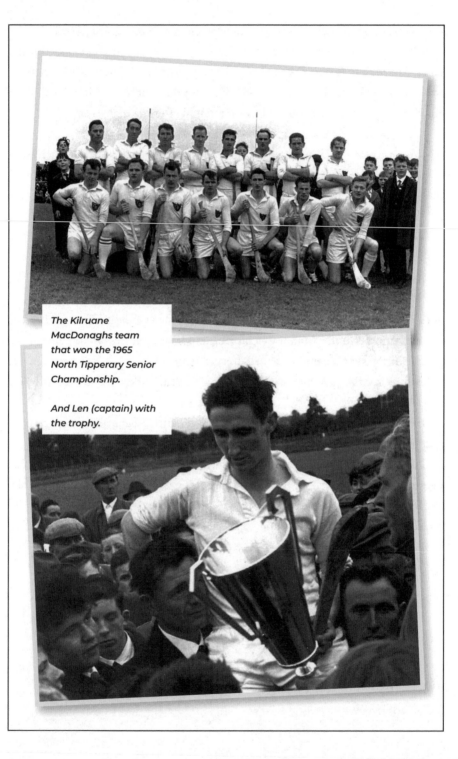

The Kilruane MacDonaghs team that won the 1965 North Tipperary Senior Championship.

And Len (captain) with the trophy.

« CHAPTER 4 »

Making the Grade

AFTER THE MUNSTER under-21 semi-final win over Clare in 1964, I received another letter from Tipperary County Board, this time inviting me to train with the senior team.

Before my first training session we had played Waterford in that Munster under-21 final where I sustained my broken wrist.

After just being called up to the Tipp senior panel it was killing me not being able to join in fully. I couldn't train as my wrist was in plaster up to my shoulder, but I still went to training and when the boys were gone out hurling, I togged out with my arm in a sling.

The minute the running part started, I ran out of the tunnel and into the group, and ran away with the lads.

Paddy Leahy was the head man that time.

'YOUNG GAYNOR!' he roared.

'YOUNG GAYNOR... COME BACK HERE!!'

I let on I didn't hear him. I was pure eager to be there and be part of it.

And Paddy didn't say a thing to me afterwards.

THE FIRST EVENING I could train properly in Thurles, there was a very tricky ball that stopped dead in the middle of the field, and I was coming out to it. And Theo English was coming the other way.

I said to myself… *This is going to be a fair one!*

Theo English was a very strong, powerful man. I never saw him on the ground, I don't think anyone ever knocked him down.

Well, I went headlong into him and neither of us fell, and I got the ball away.

I was thinking… *This is tough… but I'm still alive.*

I quickly learned how to survive.

We had great men around us such as John Doyle, Michael Maher and Kieran Carey in the full-back line; they were powerful men.

They had a reputation for being rough, tough, and dirty and were given the immortal title of "Hell's Kitchen" but they weren't really. They were tough and used their power and their weight to their advantage. Doyle loved a skirmish and pounding into lads, and the Tipperary fans loved him for it.

We came in one day after playing Cork, and this elderly supporter was in the dressing-room. How he got in I don't know. But there he was, rubbing down John Doyle. I was looking around wondering where my shirt was, and I saw it was my shirt and vest he was using to rub him down with.

John Doyle was royalty.

For us as backs, marking the likes of Jimmy Doyle, Mackey McKenna, Donie Nealon, Larry Kiely and Liam Devaney, who were all powerful hurlers, was huge. We realised we could only get better by marking them every night in training.

When you're watching those lads and seeing the things they could do, it would drive us on as well. I was raw enough going in there as a young fella. I might have been good at home in the club and thinking I had it all, but when I went to Thurles it was another step again.

The first job was to learn to survive.

◄◄◆►►

MACKEY MCKENNA

Len wasn't a big man, but he was hardy, all bone and muscle. He was great on the feet and well able to hit off both sides. He never walked into any trouble.

MICHAEL BABS KEATING
(TIPPERARY SENIOR HURLER 1964-75)

He'd be so enthusiastic in the training; he'd cut the ankles off you and I mean that in a positive sense. His enthusiasm was unbelievable, and I would have been described as lazy in those days.

◄◄◆►►

IT WAS PRETTY daunting starting out with that group of Tipperary seniors, who prior to my arrival were being touted as one of the greatest teams of all time.

Not only were they a focused team that put the work in to be as good as they were, they were also a great group of friends who looked after each other and made each new arrival on to the panel feel part of the group right from the start.

On training nights, Mackey McKenna would do the driving as he started out the furthest north, in Borrisokane. Then we would head up to Newtown for Donie Nealon and back into Nenagh to pick up Mick Burns and then on to Borrisoleigh for Liam Devaney, until he got married and moved into Thurles.

That was our load and we used to have right craic. Liam King came on the panel later and he'd be coming from Lorrha and he used to bring us then.

Mackey was a devil for the greyhounds. Himself and a man called Tom Brereton from Thurles had a greyhound between them and the deal was one of them had him for six months to keep, feed and train, and then the other would have him for the next six.

Mackey had his term completed and it was his partner's turn to take him, but he wouldn't take him as the dog was no good. We brought the dog over in the car one evening with us to training and tied it to Tom's door, and we went on to the field.

The next evening we went into training and when we came out the greyhound was tied to the door of Mackey's car, and we had to bring him home again. He must have been a real dud of a greyhound.

WHEN LIAM DEVANEY was living at home in Borrisoleigh with his parents, they reared sows and they used to sell them for a fiver apiece.

One evening, we called to Devaney's house and there was no sign of him. We were after blowing the horn for a good few minutes.

Eventually he came out.

'What the hell kept you?' Donie Nealon asked.

'The sow was having banbhs," he said.

'You and your banbhs… we have an All-Ireland to win!'

'All-Ireland me eye,' said Devaney, '… and every fart a fiver'.

◄◄◆►►

MACKEY MCKENNA

I used to have a great way with Len when we were playing Kilruane. I used to ask Len is the brother over there, as Des Gaynor used to play on the other wing. He told me he was. Is he able to dance, I asked, or does he do a tango or an old-time waltz? I knew Len was big into the dancing.

There was great banter but when the match was over it was over, and that was it.

He'd often come out with us even though he didn't drink but he'd stay out with us until three or four in the morning as he was driving the car. He was great that way. He never stopped us from having a bit of craic. He would often sing a song, but he was useless to sing… that was the craic.

I used to pity him sometimes if we were after playing a match in Cork or somewhere, and I used to say to him… 'Go on home… we'll find our own way home'. But he would never leave us stranded.

◄◄◆►►

WE WERE COMING home from Kilkenny after a league match, once, after we had been beaten. Myself, Mick Burns, Mackey McKenna, Kieran Carey, and Martin Kennedy were in Mackey's car, but I was driving because I didn't drink.

We stopped first in a pub in Urlingford. We moved on then and the boys were all asleep in the car when we got to Young's of Latteragh, a few miles from Nenagh. They had a pub and petrol pumps.

All of a shot, Mackey woke up and said, 'Pull in… pull in, we need petrol'. I pulled in and the doors shot open and the boys headed for the pub.

We got inside and there were a good few still there. I was livid because I was hoping to get into Nenagh for the last dance in the Ormond Hotel.

I wasn't even drinking water; I was sick after drinking minerals in Urlingford.

We weren't long there, when in came the Gardaí and raided the place. We were asked for our names and the first man gave a wrong name.

Then Martin Kennedy was asked for his name.

'John Shea,' says Martin.

I heard this and I thought... *We are going to go to jail.*

'Where are you from John?' asked the guard.

'Ballycommon,' said Martin.

'Ballycommon where?'

'Ballycommon, Nenagh... where do you think?' said Martin.

The next thing, Mick Burns gave me a dig in the ribs and told me to give him my right name. I felt a massive relief, hearing that, and so we all gave our names.

Some lads got out of the place through a little tiny window and Mackey McKenna saw them. You wouldn't get an eel out through it, he told us. But still a couple of lads went out through it.

We were all fined two pounds each in Nenagh Court a while later for being found on the premises after hours. It managed to make the *Evening Press* newspaper later in the week with the headline... *"Tipperary stars drown their sorrows after hours."*

AT THE END of 1964, Tipperary got to the All-Ireland final and there were 24 players on the panel, but Croke Park sent word that there would be only 20 medals. Four lads had to be dropped.

Thankfully, I kept my place.

I often think back that maybe the selection committee were impressed when I did my training when I was injured. I didn't do it for that reason, but something clicked with the manager that they kept me on, and the other lads were dropped.

I was an unused sub as Tipp beat Kilkenny in that final.

A few weeks later, we were playing Kilkenny again in the Oireachtas final at Croke Park. There was a big crowd there, around 50,000.

The All-Ireland team was picked to start again, and I was still a sub.

When we got to Croke Park, Mick Burns couldn't play; he was injured, so I was told in the dressing-room that I was playing.

Séan McLoughlin was a great leader at that time. He caught me by the front of the jersey and pinned me up against the wall. 'You're going to be marking Eddie Keher today!' he told me.

'Oh right,' says I.

'You know,' he says. 'If you stop him from scoring, we'll win this match. Do you hear me?'

'I do!' I told him.

I knew it was serious then.

I would have known a bit about Eddie Keher because he was on the St Kieran's College team that beat St Flannan's in an All-Ireland Colleges final in 1957.

I had seen him play with Kilkenny and knew he was good. I got stuck into him good and tight and didn't give him many chances. I don't know what he scored; but he scored some of the frees anyway. Sure, he was a great free-taker.

◄◄◆►►

EDDIE KEHER
(KILKENNY SENIOR HURLER 1959-77)

The first time I opposed him was in the Oireachtas final in 1964. Tipperary had beaten Kilkenny in the All-Ireland final just a few weeks previously. Len was a sub that day. I was marking Mick Burns and Tipperary annihilated us. It was probably the peak performance of that great Tipperary team.

We had won the All-Ireland final the year before that and were obviously very disappointed with our performance. The Oireachtas final was a huge competition at that time with 50,000 people at the game in Croke Park. We were anxious to redeem ourselves.

Mick Burns was injured, and Len came in to replace him and I was marking him. He was a very skilful hurler. He had great vision and was a great reader of the game. He was very good when he got possession and used it well.

He was tough as well, very strong for a slight man. In the game that time there was a lot of hip to hip clashes, with a lot of pulling and you could feel the sting going up your hurl when he pulled. He was very strong with the hurley.

His passion for the game showed in the way he played. He would have displayed all the qualities of a good hurler of that era and the way the game was played. He could have played in any era, of course, but that time hurling was tough and uncompromising. Defenders played hard and tough, and Len did that as well as play the game with honesty.

◄◄◆►►

I DIDN'T PLAY well that day as I was a little anxious, and the minute I saw the ball I was pulling on it to get rid of it.

Tony Wall was telling me to pick it up. I didn't think you'd be allowed to pick it up in county hurling.

I took a lineball under the Hogan Stand in the first-half. We were down 11 points and wave after wave of Kilkenny attacks were coming at us. I took the lineball and I got a great connection and it landed into the square, and into the net it went.

It wouldn't have gone into the net only for Séan McLoughlin, who did a war dance in front of the goals, with the ball going in between his legs and then between Ollie Walsh's legs and into the net. The goal was credited to Séan McLoughlin on the paper the next day and I was a bit disappointed.

Paddy Leahy came up to me at half-time. 'Good man young Gaynor… that was a great goal'.

That gave me a lift and I never forgot it.

It was about the first and only time I got a bit of praise. I don't ever remember getting any other praise. I really didn't play that well, I thought. I was wired anyway to stop Eddie Keher from scoring so I wouldn't be killed in the dressing-room.

At half-time, I thought there would be changes and I would be taken off. There wasn't a word said however and next thing, Theo English stood up. 'Boys… it's time we got down to business and beat these fellas.' And beat them, we did.

That's all it took to spark us. That team knew they had it in them. Nobody had to beat the table or pound the door; it was as simple as that.

I never forgot that because it was a huge message about keeping calm when things are going wrong. There was no one effing anyone else out of it. One man would tell the next man to his face if he did something wrong or didn't hit the ball right.

WE USUALLY TRAINED two nights a week and if we got to an All-Ireland it would be upped to three. It was generally Tuesdays and Fridays, and we'd hurl away. There'd be a match straight away.

I could be on Jimmy Doyle one night or Donie Nealon another... Mackey McKenna, Larry Kiely... whoever you were on you were playing against the best.

Then we'd do a few rounds of the field; then we'd do a few sprints, and that was it.

Ossie Bennett was the trainer. He was good in fairness. He was a powerful man; he drove us, and he'd drive you for that last bit of a sprint to get the most out of you.

It was completely different to nowadays.

There wasn't a lot of emphasis on training really. They would be advising you to mind yourself and eat the right stuff... whatever that was. They'd tell us to keep away from the drink.

We got good advice. We would be told how to carry ourselves as well. Maybe people would notice if lads were in a pub and having a pint, and even back then that number of pints would reach 10 by the time the story would end in different parts of the county. So, no different to now on that front, lads did have to mind themselves.

I wasn't a drinker at all, I didn't drink alcohol.

I wouldn't have had a routine, but I would make sure to keep occupied. There were a lot of farmers hurling at that time. If you went forking bales or something like that, which you might not be used to doing, you'd be murdered the next day.

But I believed that I should keep myself busy at something that I was comfortable at, whether that was out in the garden digging spuds, or something easy like that. Or painting a door... I always wanted to keep myself occupied.

There's a story about Tony Wall, who was living in Cork at one time, when he was in the Army. He had a next-door neighbour who was a big Cork supporter. Cork were going through a lean time in the 60s and this man would always feel the next year would be Cork's year. He was good friends with Tony.

Anyway, it was the 1965 Munster final between Tipp and Cork, and your man was high all day on the Saturday that they were going to beat Tipperary the next day. All day he was at it, but in the evening he went out the back door to his garden to put in a bit of time. He looked over the fence and there was Tony Wall with a mac on him, a cap and a wheelbarrow and he working away in his garden.

The man couldn't believe it and he went back in and sat down, and said to the wife, 'We are bet'... and they were beaten well the next day. He couldn't believe Tony was so calm and collected the day before a Munster final.

I WOULD HAVE trained on my own in the winter. I wouldn't have done much more during the summer apart from our own training.

Just after Christmas I'd begin to try and get myself into shape, because the league matches would be coming up pretty quickly. I remember running around the field in the dark; it wasn't dangerous, I knew where I was going!

I'd always be pucking away, and keeping my eye in at the same time. I used to go over to Lahorna ball-alley on my own with a sponge ball, which would be great to keep us sharp as well.

In later years after I was finished, I still used to go over there and Michael Cleary and Conor O'Donovan used to come out from Nenagh a good bit and I would play a game with them.

As a farmer I'd be sort of fairly fit anyway, but I felt I had to sharpen up at the same time. The little bit that I did on my own wouldn't be anything dramatic, but it was the fact that I did push myself to do it, and I was getting my mind in the right frame.

I wouldn't have been one to pack on the weight over the winter. Some of the lads did come back out of shape but they knew come championship they had to be ready, and they were.

It's a demanding game and so fast that, if you're not in shape, you're going to be left behind.

For me, preparation was also important, even the simple things. I would have the bag packed, the socks right and the boots right.

I believed in being comfortable going out, feeling good about myself; you have to feel good going out. Larry Kiely was a great man in the dressing-room because any of us could comb our hair in his boots as they were always shining. He was in the army and he taught us all about it. It is important.

It's important to have the boots right, and the socks, all those small little things make a big difference. If you are feeling comfortable, then you're probably going to give your best.

I admired all the players on the squad, many of whom had won All Irelands in 1961, '62 and then '64 when I came on to the panel.

Tony Wall was my real favourite, however.

I read about him in 1958 when he was Hurler of the Year. I liked him because of the way he played and how good he was, and how he had improved himself. When he first got on the Tipperary team, they played him wing-forward and centrefield, and eventually they dropped him into centre-back which he made his own and he stayed there for years.

He was very good to me when I went in and when I was playing beside him. He'd be encouraging me all the way; he'd never say a wrong word.

Just pure encouragement all the time.

◄◄◆►►

TONY WALL
(TIPPERARY SENIOR HURLER 1953-67)

I would have only hurled with Len fully for two or three years, but he was a hugely committed player. I worked with him and helped him the best I could, but he didn't need much help, he was well able to hold his own.

◄◄◆►►

THE BOSS, PADDY Leahy didn't say much but when he spoke, we listened.

In that first campaign with the under-21s, Paddy was brought into the dressing-room before the first match against Cork. One of the selectors said, 'This is Paddy Leahy… manager of the Tipperary senior team'.

I had heard of him but had never seen him before.

His words were magical. 'Boys, we are the Premier County. So we want to win this first All-Ireland in under-21 hurling to keep our reputation as the Premier County.' That was it and off he went.

Paddy was a very sound man. He'd speak at the last training session before a match and he would tell you what was expected of the team and different individuals, not much generally, but what the backs had to do to keep the forwards out, and for the forwards to take their chances.

He knew all about each of us. He knew if we stepped out of line, and he would let us know about it. You wouldn't last on the panel if it was anyway serious at all, you'd be gone! He knew his hurling. He was able to make all the important moves during a game, to change the flow of a game.

We trusted him and we believed in him.

He had been through it. He had been a great hurler himself having won two All-Irelands in the early decades of the century.

He didn't have the title of manager; he was chairman of the selection committee. But he was the man and we all knew he had done it before. He was there from 1949 when Tipperary's golden era began, right up to '65 when he was forced to step away due to ill health, and in that time, there was never any doubt about who was in charge.

There was never any talk of him going or being removed. There was never any question that he was going to be the man again. There might be a change in the selectors but not Paddy Leahy, he was consistent.

I admired him and I would take everything he said seriously. He was a great leader, but the dressing-room was really full of leaders.

Tony Wall was a great leader, a very wise man.

Theo English was a leader.

Séan McLoughlin was a big leader. If you ballooned a ball over McLoughlin's head he wouldn't be long in letting you know about it.

Doyle, Maher, Carey… they were leaders in their own right without saying too much.

One day before my first All-Ireland final in 1965 we were out on the field, pucking around and I remember asking Mick Maher, 'What will I do today?' I thought maybe that playing in the All-Ireland final there was something extra wanted.

'Play the game as normal,' he told me. 'Get the ball and hit it… keep it simple.'

After the Oireachtas final in 1964, I was on the senior team after that for good. I never lost my place until I retired in 1974.

By the time the National League came around in 1965, Mick Murphy had injured his knee, which finished his career, and I got to play left wing back and I stayed in the No. 7 jersey for nearly the next 10 years.

Seeing Mick finish so young was cruel. It's only now I realise it was a cruciate ligament injury that finished him, as they couldn't do anything about it at that time. I used to hear the boys saying that Murphy was playing great, but they believed that I was ready to take his place.

◄◄◆►►

DONIE NEALON
(TIPPERARY SENIOR HURLER 1958-69)

There were a lot of good hurlers that time who didn't make it, as Tipp had a very good team. Len was an excellent player but he also benefitted at that time at wing back as we lost Jimmy Finn to retirement, then we lost Michael Murphy who was forced to retire with a serious knee injury and Len got his chance, and he took it.

Len used to mark me a lot at training. That time backs marked their men. He was a very close marker, and many said he was the real steel of Tipperary even though he wasn't that big. He was very tenacious and was always going forward looking for the ball.

He'd mark you really tight; it was hard to get away from him. He was a real defender.

He was also a fine striker of the ball left and right and if you were a corner-forward when Len had the ball, you knew when to start running.

There was nothing shy about him either.

◄◄◆►►

BACK THEN, IF you lost one match in the championship you were gone, and that was it.

You'd see the difference in the lads when the league was over and they came back in for championship training.

That'd be deadly serious then.

The lads that would be drinking would stop, or they would cut it back anyway. You'd see it in them and there wouldn't be a word about it. Nobody was told not to drink or anything like that; it was taken for granted that we wouldn't.

The tempo of the training would be upped straight away.

Séan McLoughlin was a woeful man for winning, be it a tournament, anything! There was a tournament in Limerick and it had started back in Mick Mackey's time but it wasn't finished, and the medals were put away and were resurrected in the 60s. We were playing Limerick in the final of this tournament.

McLoughlin believed there were right good medals on offer. 'They were made back in the 40s and we want to win this,' he said.

This was an ordinary tournament held on Sunday evenings when everything else was over, or when we'd have been hurling earlier that day for our clubs.

WE MADE IT back to the All-Ireland final once more in 1965 where Wexford were our opponents.

I was on a fella called Jimmy O'Brien. He was a right good hurler; he was tough and hardy, and would go through you if given a chance.

One of the Wexford backs made a big clearance that went over our heads and we were both reversing back to get it. All of a sudden, Jimmy turned and faced the other way and I stayed reversing, and my hand went back and I lost track of the ball. It landed in my hand, back near my shoulders for good luck, and I cleared it up the field and Liam Devaney scored a point.

If I hadn't caught it Jimmy O'Brien would have latched on to it and ran in for a goal.

It was the only time I ever caught a ball without being able to see it, but it was a great feeling, to feel it landing in the hand.

We won the final 2-16 to 0-10, winning Tipperary's fourth All-Ireland title in five years. Séan McLoughlin was powerful that day scoring the two goals.

It was an amazing feeling not only to break into such a great team, but also to win an All-Ireland senior medal in the process.

Wexford were always a physically strong team. Their team in 1965 were a bit young and when they beat us in '68, they had matured quite a bit.

Kilkenny would always have smashing hurlers. They'd always get the ball in their hand and if you let them get it in their hand, you might not see it again because they were able to shield it and get their shot in.

Limerick would have been different. They would have been tough, dour, and strong, without any stars at the time to bring them through. Clare would have been more or less the same. They'd give you a good match for half an hour, and then you'd more than likely win.

Waterford had gone back a bit. They had a great team from 1959 to '63. The best of those lads were gone. The likes of Tom Cheasty was still there, and I played against him, he was a very forceful hurler.

They all had their own styles, different styles but basically it was getting the ball in your hands and hitting it, instead of picking out men like nowadays.

I CAME UP against great players. As I mentioned earlier, I was never afraid of playing on anyone no matter how good they were. However, the lads that beat me were lads I didn't rate highly because I wouldn't wind myself up enough.

I could lift myself for really good players.

One Sunday I was working in AI on a farm. I was tipping away and there was a match on the radio between Cork and Waterford in the Munster Championship, and we were playing the winners.

Michael O'Hehir was going mad on the commentary, raving about this new lad on the Cork team, Séanie Barry, who was scoring all around him. Then it dawned on me that he was playing on my wing. I was geared up well and I knew I had to be, or he would walk all over me.

When it came to the game, and the referee was going to throw in the ball, I was watching my man like a hawk. I knew I had to lay down a marker.

Séanie Barry came running into his position for the start and stuck out his hand to me, which was unusual at the time, as you would not shake hands before the match.

I stuck out my hand and I caught him, and gave it a little tug.

As the ball was thrown in, Barry was coming around from behind me and didn't the ball break between us but I had the yard on him, and as he was just going to put down his hand to catch the ball, I let fly and cleared it down the field.

I knew I had him then. When you win the first ball, you are in with a good chance of winning the battle.

Len in action against Wexford's Jimmy O'Brien in the 1965 All-Ireland final.

« CHAPTER 5 »

A Full Life

BETWEEN WORK AND hurling, I did also have a social life and in late 1968 I got married to Eileen O'Donoghue.

We met at a concert about four years before in Ardcroney Hall; I was 20 and Eileen was 19.

Even though we were living in the same parish we had never even seen each other, let alone met each other, before that night. She would have gone to school in Ardcroney and I went to school in Kilruane. It was like the other end of the world.

Maybe it was my love of dancing that caught her eye!

EILEEN GAYNOR

I would have known about him as we used to go to all the club matches in Borrisokane and Nenagh, even though it was all girls in my family. We were all interested in hurling.

Whether he was a good hurler or not wouldn't have meant an awful lot at that time.

I used to go to the dances in the Ormond Hotel and sometimes he would be back before the dance would be over and sometimes, he wouldn't be, including the night they were caught in the pub in Latteragh.

We went on our honeymoon up the north west of the country and I always remember when we were crossing the border from Donegal into Northern Ireland, and this guy

asked Len, 'Why aren't you playing with Tipp today?' Tipperary were playing Offaly
in Birr, but they recognised him up there.

Hurling always came first and I always understood that.

◄◄◆►►

WE WERE MARRIED on October 3, 1968, seven weeks after the All-Ireland final loss to Wexford. A year later, on October 18, we were expecting our first child, but things didn't go to plan.

Eileen had gone full term, but she wasn't feeling well and was sent to the Coombe Hospital in Dublin. Unfortunately, when they did some tests, they found that there was no heartbeat and our baby was dead. He had died less than 24 hours before.

It was devastating.

The matron showed me the little baby boy in a little wicker basket. We called him Patrick. I started to cry when I saw him. Eileen was still in the bed; she didn't know at that stage that Patrick had died.

The obstetrician, Dr J.J. Stuart hit me a punch into the chest and said, 'Don't you let your wife see you crying like that'.

I had to try and be the strong man.

It wasn't easy, there weren't supports for bereaved families at that time. Nowadays there are people that will help you in that situation in the hospital and they'll be available. They would help you out and help you to understand, but we had no one.

I was the one that had to tell Eileen that Patrick was dead. Eileen was devastated after all her great work for nine months and here we were going home with the baby clothes with us, but no baby.

The matron then asked me would she take care of the burial and I said to go ahead, which was a mistake. I thought about it after. We have a graveyard beside our own land where we could have brought the baby home and buried him there, but we didn't and by the time we realised, it was too late and Patrick had already been buried.

I couldn't think straight at the time as no one gave us any idea of what to do after losing a baby. Unfortunately, it was the norm at the time.

It took us another 15 years to find out where Patrick was buried. Now we didn't look in a hurry, but we started to enquire after a while and when we did, we found out he was buried in Glasnevin cemetery. They had an account of the birth, death and the burial, and his name is on his grave to this day. That was a big help.

◄◄◆►►

EILEEN GAYNOR

That was the worst year of our lives. Tipp were beaten in the Munster final by Cork in Limerick and that team were described as one of the most spiritless teams that ever went down.

Len got a tiny scratch in his arm which became infected and he spent three weeks in Croom Hospital, and I travelled down every day to see him. And when he came home, he was another three weeks in plaster.

In October, we were expecting our first baby. I was fortunate that Dr J.J. Stuart, who was president of the GAA from 1958 to 1961, was my obstetrician.

I was with Dr Stuart in the Coombe Hospital on October 11 and was scheduled to come in to have the baby on October 24.

Len went training on the Friday night and when he came home, I didn't feel well, and he took me into Nenagh hospital and his mother came with us.

I used to attend Dr Lemass in Nenagh but he wasn't available and the locum wasn't around either but the nurse was concerned that she couldn't feel any life but they didn't say anything to me or Len at that stage.

I was told to go by car to the Coombe in Dublin. However, the car broke down in Newbridge. I always remember O'Connor's newsagents in Newbridge; we borrowed a lamp to help get the car going again and when we were coming back home 10 days later, we called back in to give back the lamp. I have never forgotten that shop.

We got to the hospital at about seven o'clock in the morning and I was in labour. At that time, the husband wasn't allowed into the delivery room with the wife. At that time too, the policy was that the hospital took care of the burial. I never saw Patrick as I was sedated for three days, but Len and his mother did.

I always remember Dr Stuart coming in and putting his arms around me. 'We'll take care of the burial,' he said. We were pure green; we could have brought our baby home to our own graveyard which is right across from our house.

He was buried in Glasnevin and it wasn't until 1984 that we found out where.

That was a milestone in our lives, December 6, 1984.

It was also the day I got involved with a support group called ISANDS at the time. To this day, I am still involved with that group who are now called A Little Lifetime Foundation.

It was tough. People didn't know what to say. They were different times. The selectors did come to the house to sympathise, but hurling was Len's salvation really.

The grief of fathers is now very much recognised but at that time it wasn't. People would ask Len… 'How is your wife?'

But they would never ask him… 'How are you?'

◄◄◆►►

LIFE WENT ON and two weeks later, we were playing Kilkenny in the league and I was in no shape to hurl at all, but the selectors persuaded me to play.

I blanked out everything in my mind and played as best I could. I can only remember one incident in the match, right at the end. I don't know how I played, but Eddie Keher got a 21-yard free to win the match. To stop a 21-yard free you have to get a glimpse of the ball but Keher had a devastating way of taking a '21'. He would go back four or five yards and he'd run up very fast with short sharp steps and rise the ball in full flight, and let fly.

To try and get a glimpse of the ball was nearly impossible.

But I got a glimpse at the last second and I saved it. Someone else cleared it as I was stunned, it had come so hard at me.

We won the match and I went into the dressing-room after and the dam burst, and I started crying my eyes out.

The boys didn't know what was wrong and wondered who had hit me?

That game was what released the tension that was in me and the disappointment of losing my first child. That was a really tough time.

Thankfully in 1970, Eamonn was born on September 29.

It was a very nervous time, but they performed a caesarean section to make sure everything would be okay. Actually, he was the spitting image of Patrick, it was unbelievable.

PEOPLE DIDN'T KNOW what to say to us, whether to sympathise or not; they just didn't know, it was no fault of anyone's. Those things weren't talked about at that time.

But December 6, 1984 was a turning point for us when we visited Glasnevin Cemetery. From then on, Eileen got involved with ISANDS, travelling the length and breadth of the country with two local members, Pauline and Mary. They helped to arrange support meetings and memorial services.

ISANDS campaigned for 10 years to the government to have a stillbirth register established. Prior to 1995, a stillbirth was not recognised by the State, causing much anguish to bereaved parents. It was a proud day for Eileen and the members, as they sat in the Dáil gallery to hear the Minister for Equality and Law Reform, Mervyn Taylor pass the law to allow parents to obtain a certificate of stillbirth.

Not only this, but the law was made retrospective, the only law of its kind at the time, meaning that parents who were bereaved previously could now register their stillbirth baby, irrespective of how long ago it had happened.

HURLING WENT ON, but earlier in 1969 I almost came a cropper.

I got a belt on my left elbow in a Munster final against Cork in Limerick, which we lost 4-6 to 0-9. It bled a little but it wasn't serious.

We went into the dressing-room after and I had a shower. Dressing-rooms weren't up to scratch at the time and weren't the most hygienic. I had my own towel and I dried myself down, and I stood on the towel as I dressed myself.

I was putting on my shirt, and someone said, 'Mind your shirt… there's blood on your elbow!'

He picked up the towel off the dirty wet floor and wiped the blood off.

I put on my shirt and went away home.

The next day the elbow was sore, but I didn't think anything of it and assumed it would go away in a few days.

On the Tuesday I could hardly move and I went to Dr Louis Courtney in Nenagh. He said there was a bone resting on a nerve.

'I'm sending you to Croom Hospital straight away… don't even go home! he told me.

I was shaking at the time; I didn't know what was going on.

I got a colleague, John Lee, who worked with the AI and asked him to drive me to Croom. We had the heaters on in the car going down despite it being the month of July. It was quite warm, but I had his overcoat on and was still shaking.

I went into the hospital and they asked what was wrong, and I said I didn't know. I had forgotten about the cut on the elbow, and didn't think anything of it.

I became delirious in bed and I fell asleep. I woke up the next morning and the doctor was standing over me and he said, 'Only for the penicillin last night… you were dead.'

He said an infection had gone right through me. My arm was put in a sling and plastered from my wrist to my elbow. I was in hospital for three weeks and had the plaster on for another three weeks after coming home.

I couldn't go back working with the AI, I couldn't do anything, never mind hurling.

That was a raw, tough time after being beaten in that Munster final.

Eileen was expecting Patrick then and she drove down to Croom every day to see me. I can't remember how I was after that, but I know I was weak for a good while afterwards. I was shook, very shook.

I felt bad about it as well, because no one bothered about me. I wasn't of interest to anyone, because we weren't in the championship. I felt sore about that as well but that was the way life was at that time; you looked after yourself and that was it.

IN 1971, WE were back in the All-Ireland final and Eileen was expecting again, this time with Fionnuala. The doctor was going to induce her. He didn't want her going full term.

So, they wanted Eileen in the Coombe the day before the final. She asked if she could go to the match and come in immediately afterwards, and they agreed, so she was at the All-Ireland final in 1971 and she was as big as 'Borris'.

A priest walked by Eileen and he thought to himself… *That woman should not be here.*

Anyway, she went into hospital immediately after seeing us win the final against Kilkenny, but it was the following day before Fionnuala was born.

There was a photo taken of us with the baby, and it appeared in the national papers the following day and the priest at the match who made the comment saw the photo and he came into the Coombe to see us and he said, 'I saw you at the match and I didn't think you should be there'.

He was delighted to meet Eileen, and he brought her flowers as well.

◄◄◆►►

EILEEN GAYNOR

I asked Dr Stuart could I go to the All-Ireland and he said I could. 'Sure I will be there anyway, if anything happens,' he told me.

Len went to Dublin with the team on the Saturday night, and I went up on the Sunday morning. I dropped my case into the Coombe and had lunch there with Len's mother and his sister, Imelda, who nursed there. Then we went on to Croke Park for the match.

After the match was over, I never went near Len to congratulate him. I went straight back to the Coombe and into the nurses' dining-room for my tea and discovered that Dr Stuart had been in looking for me.

There was a planned delivery the next day and he left instructions that I was to be induced at six o'clock the next morning as he wanted to get the birth over before Len went home with the team.

On the front page of the Irish Press *on the Monday, Peadar O'Brien had written,* "Another star for Tipperary?"

Len and Babs Keating had come in to see me in the hospital that Sunday night and word got back to the banquet that I was in hospital, so that's how Peadar O'Brien got the story.

Fionnuala wasn't born until 6.45pm on the Monday evening when Len was at the train station seeing the team off, so he came back to the hospital and stayed the night. The Evening Press *were in the next morning for the photo.*

Len and Eileen were married on October 3, 1968 and (right) celebrate the birth of Fionnuala in September 1971. And Len and Eileen with their young family in 1982 (Eamonn, Fionnuala, Brian and, (front), Lennie, Ciara, Sinéad and Eimear).

« CHAPTER 6 »

Bedding into the Team

GOING INTO 1966, this group of Tipperary players had never won a three in-a-row of All-Ireland senior titles and a lot of the boys were keen to make up for what happened in '63 when they were previously going for the same record and were stunned by Waterford in the Munster final.

It was a day when nothing went right for them; when every Waterford chance seemed to find the target while for Tipperary, they couldn't hit a barn door from 10 paces.

The team stayed together for 1966 but we crucially lost one key component, Paddy Leahy.

We would have known he was sick as the day of the 1965 Oireachtas final against Kilkenny, a few weeks after the All-Ireland final, he watched from the stand.

However, he made his way into the dressing-room at half-time as we were awful in the first-half, and were trailing 1-6 to 0-2. He was a frail man at this stage but his influence on the group was huge and we knew we had let this great man down in the opening half.

He said a few words and there was a sense that this would be his final outing as the head of the Tipperary senior team.

When he left the dressing-room, we were very quiet for a few seconds, until Kieran Carey stood up and asked us all one question.

'Are we going to let that man down?'

Leahy's presence was the kick up the backside we needed and in the second-half we blitzed Kilkenny 2-10 to 1-1 to win by five points, completing the year as All-Ireland, Munster, National League and Oireachtas champions.

SHORTLY BEFORE THE start of the 1966 championship, Paddy died in May at the age of 74.

We struggled to get things going that year. It was our own fault. Whether it was down to not having Paddy in charge, I don't know.

Paddy Ryan 'Sweeper' from Moycarkey, who was already on the selection committee, took over as chairman. He didn't change much from Paddy Leahy, but he wouldn't have carried the same influence as Paddy; nobody would have carried the same influence as Paddy.

A week after Paddy's death, we were defeated by Kilkenny in the National League final, the first time in 44 years that Tipperary were defeated by Kilkenny in a national final.

Following that we only had two weeks to prepare for the first round of the Munster Championship against Limerick.

A lot of guys didn't play that day. Tony Wall was on a tour of duty that year with the UN in Cyprus and was a big loss at centre-back, with John Gleeson moved from full-back to centre-back to fill in while Mick Roche, Larry Kiely and Jimmy Doyle missed the game through injury also. Mackey McKenna and Séan McLoughlin weren't fully fit having just come back from injury and illness respectively.

Limerick were an emerging team, with Éamon Cregan and Eamon Grimes coming on stream. They were lively and we were caught flat-footed. I got the first score of the game which was unusual for a back man at that time, but it didn't lead to anything as we were beaten 4-12 to 2-9

COMING INTO 1967, this Tipperary team was starting to move on. Full-back, Michael Maher retired after the 1966 campaign, but the rest stayed on and Tony Wall had returned from abroad.

It was a big year, as I knew it was going to be the last campaign for some of the lads such as Kieran Carey and John Doyle, so I was driven to win this one for these lads and let them finish on a high. I prepared diligently and felt I was in good shape going into the championship.

We defeated Waterford in the Munster semi-final before facing Clare in the final at the Gaelic Grounds. It proved to be Jimmy Smith's last chance of trying for a Munster medal with Clare, but Tipp had too much class and won 4-12 to 2-6, holding Clare to just two points in the second-half.

We progressed straight to the All-Ireland final. There was also a lot of hullabaloo about John Doyle going to break Christy Ring's record and win his ninth All-Ireland medal. Doyle didn't want any noise at all about it. All he wanted to do was to go out and hurl and win.

I felt very strongly about it, that we should win it, that all these lads were coming to the end of their careers.

The newspapers kept bringing it up. Doyle wouldn't be bothered one way or another, but it was there, and it was built up into a big thing. And the next thing it became *the* thing.

It would motivate the opposition as well, not to let him get the ninth. I felt very strongly about it that we had to win. I wouldn't have noticed we had dropped our standards a bit, whether other people had noticed our performance, I don't know.

We didn't train extremely hard for the final. The management were shielding the older lads so as not to kill them and have them fresh. I thought it was a mistake.

You wouldn't fault the management or anything like that. I would have felt we didn't push ourselves enough in training and that was it, we were beaten.

We were leading 2-6 to 1-3 at half-time but Kilkenny got on top at midfield in the second-half and provided the service for their forwards to take over. They won, 3-8 to 2-7, holding us to a meagre one point in the second period.

Unfortunately, Father Time had caught up with most of the team with Dermot Gilleese in his report in the *Daily Mail* writing:

"Kilkenny proved beyond all doubt that hurling is a young man's game. The bitter truth which Tipperary must now face is that they had little chance of winning their 22nd title with eight players over 30 in the side, and the result was that their oldest player, John Doyle, was deprived of a record ninth All-Ireland title."

I ALWAYS TOOK it hard when I lost any game. You would remember them more than the matches you won. But I got over them quickly, there's no point in dwelling on them. In a day or two they'd be gone and I'd be looking forward to next year. We were naturally disappointed, but we didn't deserve to win as Kilkenny were much the better team.

The dressing-room was gloomy with no one able to say anything or have any words of comfort. I was quiet enough in the room but in later years I might have had something to say. Overall, I usually kept my own counsel.

In terms of the game, I felt that I had played fairly well.

But I was very disappointed to have lost. Disappointment, however, turned to devastation the following morning when word emerged that Tom Walsh, who had played centre-forward for Kilkenny, had lost an eye and would never play again. He was 23 at the time.

Winning or losing has little importance in the face of such personal tragedy. I did not know that Tom had been injured or had left the field, I was so focused on my own game. When the match was over we started to hear rumours that he had an eye injury.

We heard that night, at the Tipperary Association dinner, that the injury was serious. It was only the following morning at a function for both teams that the Kilkenny secretary announced that Tom had lost his eye.

We were all devastated.

I feel the need to say that I have spoken more than once to the Tipperary player involved in the incident which resulted in the injury, and I believe that the injury was totally accidental and, indeed, continued to be a real source of sadness for the player involved. This player was always a most honourable hurler and would never play a dirty stroke.

Tom Walsh was a brilliant hurler.

He had won three All-Ireland minor titles with Kilkenny and he was their brightest young star at the time. He was very fast, very accurate and a great all-round hurler. He generally played wing forward but, that year, they played him at centre-forward.

He was a grave loss to Kilkenny hurling, and to spectators who admired his style and class.

UNFORTUNATELY, THE ATMOSPHERE that developed following the injury to Tom Walsh carried over into the 1968 campaign where Tipp and Kilkenny met again in the National League final at Croke Park, and while we won 3-9 to 1-13, the game was remembered for all the wrong reasons.

The game was fairly hot and heavy, bordering on nasty at times. The newspapers got hold of it and they said something had to be done to clean up hurling.

As a result of the referee's report on the game, Central Council appointed an investigating committee to examine the incidents. The findings were not announced until early July, by which time the championship was underway, and it resulted in six-month suspensions for Tipperary's John Flanagan as well as Kilkenny's Ollie Walsh.

Following the verdict, Tipperary County Board discussed the findings and issued a very strong statement of dissatisfaction:

"The board expresses its dissatisfaction at the severity of the sentences imposed on both players and is also solid in its condemnation of all national press reports of the game.

"It also feels that the press reports created a climate of public opinion which helped in no small way to encourage Central Council to arrive at their decision."

Tipperary's response, ahead of the 1968 All-Ireland final against Wexford, was to refuse attendance to six journalists to the media night ahead of the final – John D Hickey and Donal Carroll of the *Irish Independent*; Mick Dunne, Gerry McCarthy and Padraig Puirseil of the *Irish Press* and Paddy Downey of *The Irish Times*.

That didn't go down well and the National Union of Journalists responded by refusing to print news or match reports on Tipperary matches until such time as good relations between the county board and the media were restored. The affair lingered on until the end of the year.

Off the back of the fallout from the game, some new rules were brought in to clean up the game, banning third-man tackles, and insisting you couldn't tackle straight into the body and had to go shoulder-to-shoulder.

THAT 1967 ALL-IRELAND final victory was a turning point in the rivalry between Tipperary and Kilkenny, which was decidedly one way traffic for around half a century beforehand.

Kilkenny were generally tagged for lacking the toughness to go with their skill until then and I maintain that when Pat Henderson came into the team at centre-back, he was the man that put the steel into them. He was a strong, hard man and he put a lot of bottle into the rest of the Kilkenny team.

They did change. They were very stylish up to that but then in 1967 and '68 they put extra steel into themselves. That was really *the* difference and the new rules came in and the game loosened up quite a bit after that.

It was always physical anyway. If you played Cork in a Munster final, you'd know it was physical, all these big games were physical – at the time it was a very physical game, and it is still but not to the same degree.

You had to use your body; there was plenty of shouldering that time and if you got a belt you had to take it and stay going. You just left it on the field and you forgot about it, and you got to work on again the next day.

But there was a little bit of bitterness in the air, you'd feel the atmosphere being different when we played Kilkenny, but thankfully that has all died away now. There is serious rivalry still but there is no real bitter stuff there.

◄◄◆►►

EDDIE KEHER

The matches between Tipperary and Kilkenny that time were really tough encounters. There was always great rivalry between Tipperary and Kilkenny as neighbouring counties, but the phrase was that time that Kilkenny were the hurlers and Tipperary were the men, and when it came to a big match Kilkenny could not beat them.

Come 1967, Kilkenny had built a physically strong team to match Tipperary, so it was fire against fire then and it was bound to spill over, which it did in the 1968 league final.

It was definitely a carry-over from the 1967 All-Ireland final. We matched them physically up to a point, but we had beaten Tipp at last in a final for the first time in 45 years. So, having beaten them, Tipp would have been keen to come back and re-establish themselves again and we didn't stand back from them and it spilled over, unfortunately. The first-half of that league final thankfully was the end of that bitterness. It wasn't very pleasant to be part of or for anyone watching it.

DESPITE THE LIKES of John Doyle, Kieran Carey, Tony Wall and Theo English heading into retirement, we still reached the All-Ireland final in 1968 with many of the players that backboned the '64 under-21 All-Ireland winning team.

However, there wasn't anyone as big to replace the men we had lost. The big names were gone and you could feel that, no disrespect to the likes of John Costigan, Noel O'Gorman, John Gleeson and the Ryan brothers from Carrick Davins, PJ and Jimmy, who came into the team. The shoes to fill were huge.

Conor O'Dwyer, who worked in the bank in Borrisokane for a while, from Thurles Sarsfields, was a powerful centre-back but there was no opening there for him as Tony Wall was there but by the time Wall retired, O'Dwyer was past his best.

I played at centre-back against Waterford in the first round. I was on Tom Cheasty; he was still hanging on in there from the great Waterford team of '59.

I wasn't comfortable at centre-back, I felt I wasn't big enough to command the area. I was better off on the wing and I liked the wing as well, so I was back there for the next match.

It was Mick Roche who got the No.6 jersey. He was a powerful hurler. I always maintain he was a better midfielder than a centre-back because he could control the whole show from there, as Noel McGrath does today.

He knew where to be and was a great man to read the game; his stick-work was just immaculate, he could do anything with the ball.

It was hard to break into the forward line also because you couldn't drop the established lads, because they were still the best we had. Liam Devaney was a sub some days but that was fairly rare. He wouldn't mind, but he was good enough to be on always and that's the way the selectors saw it.

WITH THE RIVALRY that built up between ourselves and Kilkenny from the 1967 All-Ireland final and the National League final in '68, we were a little disappointed that when it came to the All-Ireland later that year, it wasn't Kilkenny that were facing off against us, but Wexford.

We had defeated Clare in the Munster semi-final before beating Cork in the provincial final in Limerick, with Babs Keating superb that day, scoring 1-3.

We were expected to win the final but we were fooled a little bit as we beat Wexford easily in the 1965 All-Ireland with much the same team. We forgot they had matured a good bit since. They were very young then, now they were three years older.

We had them on the rack. We were beating them well by eight points at half-time (1-11 to 1-3) and it looked as if we were going to win but we lost our drive in the second-half. We thought we were nearly there.

◄◄◆►►

MICHAEL BABS KEATING

1968 was a disaster and going in at half-time we were leading by eight points. I remember Donie Nealon saying to me, 'All-Irelands can't be won this easy!'

◄◄◆►►

ALREADY WITHOUT JOHN Flanagan through suspension, Jimmy Doyle was also playing with an ankle injury that hampered him badly and was mainly restricted to frees.

The selectors were planning on taking him off at half-time and bringing on Francis Loughnane, but they decided to leave Doyle on for the second-half as he was captain.

He wasn't able to run and it was a mistake but it was just an understandable mistake to give him every chance as he was such an important player. He did manage to finish with 1-1 from play for his troubles.

Taking him off would have been a big blow to us and would have been a big psychological lift for Wexford with our danger man gone.

But towards the end of the game when things went against us, Jimmy finally had to make way, with Francis Loughnane brought on, and he nearly turned it around himself. It was his first big day out and he made a few great runs which led to goals for Babs Keating and Seán McLoughlin as we scored 3-12, which was a huge tally back then but it wasn't enough as Wexford scored 5-8 with Jack Berry and Tony Doran bagging a brace of goals each.

However, what killed us that day was our defence, apart from Mick Roche who gave one of the greatest All-Ireland final performances at centre-back. He was a commanding figure there. It was unfortunate for him to lose and to play so well.

Wexford got a couple of goals early in the second-half with high balls dropping in on top of Tony Doran who was a young fella but a big strong man. He caught a few balls and you could hand-pass them into the net still at that stage.

They went from eight points down at half-time to eight points up, but we came back again and got a couple of goals near the end. It was all too late, however, and we weren't able to catch them. They deservedly won it.

For a county so used to having won All-Ireland finals, to have lost two finals in-a-row was new territory altogether. It was a big blow. Everything started to change; selectors would be changed every year and players were moved on, and that made it worse because there was no stability there and there was no continuity there. The thing sort of fell apart.

We got to Munster finals in 1969 and '70 and we lost them as well to a youthful Cork side on both occasions.

PADDY 'SWEEPER' RYAN moved on as chairman of selectors in 1970 when two of my old comrades, Theo English and Kieran Carey were brought into the fold alongside John Lanigan, Jimmy Hennessy and Séan Ryan. They helped guide Tipperary to the All-Ireland title in 1971, six years after our previous success which felt like an eternity in such a hurling-mad county.

That year, we beat Clare in the Munster semi-final to set up a final with Limerick, who had beaten us earlier in the year in the league final.

The final was scheduled for Killarney, which was an unusual choice as there had only been two previous hurling finals there, in 1892 and 1950.

With such a long trip to Kerry, we stayed overnight in the town in a hotel. I was packing my bag on the Friday night prior to leaving and I said to myself... *I won't be home until late Sunday night...*

I'd better make sure I have enough clothes with me.

I put in two pairs of hurling boots, including a new pair I got only a few days before. The old hurling boots were leather and were as heavy as lead. I was afraid to wear the new boots, but I threw them into the bag anyway along with a spare pair of socks and togs.

I roomed with Dinny Ryan and I was with him for the All-Ireland final as well.

Munster final day was fierce wet. When the match started it milled rain and the poor supporters were drenched. We got drowned on the field as well. Coming into the dressing-room at half-time we were losing by six points, and it wasn't looking good.

I was hardly able to lift my feet, the leather boots soaked the water in, and it had soaked into my socks. The togs were wet, the jersey was wet… everything was wet.

Luckily, I was prepared and had my spares in the bag and I put them on, and I felt like a new man going back out. I'll never forget the feeling I had when I put on these dry clothes and boots.

For the second-half it never rained at all and the sun came out. I was flying it and we all got going. We beat Limerick by only a point in the end with John Flanagan getting the winning score in a 4-16 to 3-18 win. It was a tough struggle though.

◄◄◆►►

RICHIE BENNIS
(LIMERICK SENIOR HURLER 1965-75)

I marked Len in the 1971 league final and the Munster final below in Killarney late the same year. That Munster final was one of Len's best ever performances. I scored 13 points the same day, but I was only on him for a quarter of an hour.

He was very committed and honest. He didn't give away much. He really played from the heart. He had a very sharp pull; he would have pulled twice before you pulled twice. His lack of size demanded it.

He was very quick to whip. He wouldn't dilly-dally on the ball. He would have been a timber-merchant, but I mean that in a positive sense.

That's the way it was, you had to mind yourself. You couldn't go stupidly blindly into a fella pulling on a ball as you had no helmet to protect yourself.

He was able to dish it out and was arrogant enough in a good way when you confronted it. Most players of his calibre were gentlemen off the field.

TIPPERARY WENT ON to the All-Ireland semi-final against Galway in Birr. John Connolly was playing for Galway and played very well. Mick Roche was on him and he played very well also. We put up a big score, 3-27 and won fairly well in the end, but also conceded 6-8 and went on to Croke Park to face Kilkenny again in the 1971 All-Ireland final.

It was a reasonable game despite the high scoring nature of it where we won 5-17 to 5-14 in what was the first 80-minute final. It was fairly hectic.

It was the first time we played that length of a match. I was jaded in the last 10 minutes as it was 20 minutes extra – it jumped from 60 minutes to 80 minutes before it came back to 70 minutes eventually, but the way it is now it is nearly 80 minutes.

We got a fairly lucky goal from Noel O'Dwyer to get us going. Ollie Walsh let one in that he should have saved and we went on from there. We were well in control. John Flanagan, Roger Ryan (two) and Dinny Ryan scored goals near the end but we let Kilkenny back into it; Eddie Keher scored a couple of goals from frees, and Kieran Purcell scored another blistering goal but we held on with Babs putting on a show, despite playing in his bare feet for a time as his boots were hurting him and he couldn't run properly.

It was such a relief to win that game after losing the previous two finals. All the great players had gone. This was virtually a new team on their own, bar the likes of myself, Babs Keating, Mick Roche and Jimmy Doyle, who came on as a sub in his last All-Ireland final. Noel O'Dwyer starred at centre-back with the Roscrea trio of Roger Ryan, Francis Loughnane, and a young Tadhg O'Connor in their pomp.

Funnily enough, despite a lot of promise, that team never lined out together again and wouldn't win another All-Ireland title.

In the middle of his Tipperary career, Len met with triumph and disappointment. Here he is with Eileen on March 16, 1968 at the celebration dinner after winning a Cú Chulainn award (pre-All Stars). Also photographed are teammates, Mick Roche and Noel O'Gorman.

Len with the great RTÉ commentator, Michael O'Hehir outside Wembley Stadium in 1973.

« CHAPTER 7 »

Facing a Famine

AFTER 1971, THINGS started to go downhill for Tipperary hurling, and it lasted for much of the next 20 years.

We didn't do much in 1972, losing our only championship match to Cork in the Munster semi-final, but we did play an infamous league match against the Rebels later that year which ended in controversy.

Liam King was struck dangerously under a high ball by two Cork players. We all saw red and everyone was gunning to get the culprit as the match went on.

When the match was over there was a big row, which I got involved in too. The Cork lads were coming off the field and the crowd were booing and baying for blood. I stood in front of the Cork players at the entrance to the tunnel, and defied them to come in past me.

The upshot of it all was that an investigation took place and we were all called to Croke Park. We were in one room, and the Cork lads were next door. The atmosphere wasn't too nice.

We were called in to give evidence and there were three ex-Presidents there hearing us, along with Ard Stiúrthóir, Seán Ó Síocháin.

The Tipp players had agreed beforehand that we wouldn't name any names or blame anyone from Cork. We were called in individually and we all gave the same story.

But the funny thing was we heard the Cork lads going in and we could also hear them through the wall, and they were singing like canaries. We could hear them naming what certain Tipperary players did. We were disappointed with that.

Liam King ended up being suspended for 12 months, as well as Cork's Pat Hegarty and Seamus Power. Babs Keating was also banned for four months and the county board were fined £100, which was a substantial amount of money at the time.

Again, the county board weren't happy with the punishments handed out and said the suspensions were "barbarous and unjustified" but after several appeals, the decisions were upheld.

1973 WAS MY last full year playing for Tipperary. We defeated Waterford in the first round in Munster before scoring five goals in the semi-final to upset Cork.

We reached a Munster final in Thurles but lost to an infamous last gasp '70' from Richie Bennis as Limerick won and would go on and win the All-Ireland, their last until the 2018 success.

The controversial nature of that score overshadowed the game, though we didn't deserve to win. We let in six goals and you can't win games doing that.

We didn't play well but we were still in the running and were level in the final minute and they got a '70'. However, we argued that the ball had last come off a Limerick player.

Referee, Mick Slattery told Richie Bennis this was the last puck of the game and he had to score directly. As a left wing back, I usually stood with my back to the left goal post. I always watched that corner for any long frees to give the goalie a handout.

Richie Bennis took the '70' and it was coming towards me and it was inside the post about two feet, but then it started to lose momentum and started to drift to the left and it drifted out, four inches wide of the left post.

That is for certain.

◄◄◆▷►

RICHIE BENNIS

I was at the funeral of a Brother Dwan, who was a native of Kilruane but spent a lot of time in Adare and I had great time for him. I met Len there and the first thing he said was, 'That was wide'.

That is always the first salute I get from Len when I meet him.

◄◄◆►►

THE NEXT THING the umpire reached for the white flag and he put it up; it was a point. I couldn't believe it and I gave him a jab of the hurley which I shouldn't have.

I'd say the referee wasn't keen to make an issue of it. He was told by his umpire what I did and the Munster Council tried their best to get to the bottom of it, even going so far as to look for the game footage from RTÉ but nothing came of it.

A funny thing happened after. I don't know how it came about but there was a challenge match organised between Clarecastle, Mick Slattery's club, and Kilruane MacDonaghs in Cloughjordan, maybe within a week of the Munster final. Mick Slattery arrived with the Clarecastle team and I met him.

'Hello Mick, you're welcome to Cloughjordan,' I told him.

'Thank you very much Len, and you have nothing to worry about,' he said.

So, I was okay.

It was one of the few times I lost my cool on a hurling field. I couldn't believe that the umpire would put up the flag. He may have got the wrong view of it; most people thought it was a point but unless you were in the right position you would not know.

If you were looking across you would think it was a point. The ball was heavier that time and it would drift. Back then it was hard to get a long puck out of it, whereas nowadays they are driving it way over the bar.

The white flag went up anyway and that was it, we were beaten by a point. I couldn't believe it. Another Munster final gone, another All-Ireland final gone.

We might not have won them, but we should have been still in it.

YOU ALWAYS THINK in Tipperary that you have a chance to win an All-Ireland. Every year you go out, you feel if we do our business right, we should be able to win it. I always thought that way anyway. I didn't expect to win them all, but I felt it was possible to win.

I knew I was slowing up a little bit and when that starts to happen, the confidence goes, and it was starting to creep up on me. I didn't realise it quickly enough, but the selectors did.

The chopping and changing of selectors wouldn't have helped, either. Anyway, I couldn't complain, I had 10 good years and I was happy enough I had done my best.

I played in the early rounds of the National League in the autumn of 1973, but I was gone from the panel for the championship of '74.

It was through the daily paper that I found out the Tipperary panel that would start training for the championship and my name wasn't on it, and like that I was gone. No letter, no phone call to say I was dropped, nothing! That was it.

I didn't know I was in trouble, but the team were playing poorly, and I knew there were going to be changes and I was one of the oldest, so it was fairly obvious.

John Gleeson from Moneygall was dropped as well. Paddy Maher, a fellow Moneygall man and the secretary of the North board went to town over it. It was wrong really but you have to take your medicine.

You'd love to be still playing. You still think you were able to play, it wouldn't have dawned on me that I might be slowing down.

I knew I wouldn't get back on the panel. I didn't expect to get back, really; the management made their choice and that was it.

And just like that, 10 years of county hurling was over. It just flew by, but I accepted my time was up pretty easily.

I always looked on hurling as a sort of liberation. When you went out on to the field, you had to do your own thing. You had all the instructions and the coaching, but when you crossed the white line you had to decide whether you were going for this ball or you weren't, or whether you were going to catch it or strike it.

I always loved that part of it as you were a free agent when you went out on the field. You weren't going to school. There was no homework, no farm work… no nothing, you were hurling and you had no one telling you what to do.

You were your own man and I found it liberating, a terrific game to be able to play.

I loved playing and I got a great kick out of it, either win or lose. I was able to take my beating. I'd be sorry and disappointed alright, but I could take it. I would always congratulate the winners and I meant it.

THE JOY OF hurling was something that really gripped me from an early age and it stayed with me all the time. And I was delighted; it was an honour to be able to play for Tipperary and to win a fair bit. It was a lovely career.

I would love to be still hurling. I miss it a lot but obviously looking back now I can say that when I could hurl, I did hurl. And I gave it my best shot all of the time.

You had to be at your best as you had to play against the best. Eddie Keher was one of the best I came across, he was blisteringly fast. A great hurler with a great hurling brain. He knew where to be, and you had to be alert to hold him.

Jimmy O'Brien of Wexford was a good hurler, a very hard hurler. You wouldn't hear much about him now, but he was a great opponent. Séanie Barry and Gerald McCarthy of Cork, Eamon Grimes and Richie Bennis of Limerick, they were powerful hurlers.

Clare then had Liam Danagher who was a good hurler. Pat Cronin was good as well, but he played mostly on the other wing.

In Waterford, I played on Tom Cheasty once and he would have been too strong for me, and he was coming near the end at that stage. They had a marvellous team in 1959 when they won the All-Ireland. I was at that game against Kilkenny.

During my county career, I was also fortunate to line out in the blue of Munster in the inter-provincial championships, or the Railway Cup as they were at the time.

This competition was bigger before my time, but it was starting to wane a little bit when I played in the late 60s and now has been disbanded altogether.

It was still a great honour to be selected. You were playing with strangers on the hurling field and you were also playing against the very best. It was a challenge.

Bad weather nearly finished the Railway Cups with people not willing to go out in the cold and rain to see them.

Also, the big stars were gone. Christy Ring, John Doyle, they were the big draw. There would be trains and buses going and they'd see all the stars together, the likes of Jimmy Smith of Clare, who never won an All-Ireland, but was on Railway Cup teams. He was a great hurler, and himself and Ring used to be in the full-forward line and were virtually unbeatable.

It started to wane a little when people became more mobile and were seeing these players for their clubs and counties on the television so frequently. So, they didn't have to see them again when the Railway Cup came up.

I was delighted to have won three Railway Cups in 1968, '69 and '70 and to have played with and against the best players.

COUNTY HURLING IN the 60s also meant trips abroad. I went on a few of them, but I also skipped a few as well.

If you won the National League in Ireland back then it was called the 'Home Final'. Then you had to go to New York to win it outright by beating New York on two successive Sundays, and the overall score over the two games would determine the National League champions. We always won it. Every second year they would come to Ireland.

We used to get 21 days in New York to play those matches. It was a great holiday.

I would never have been in New York only for it. I got my fill of it as well.

Back in the 60s, the Irish in New York tended to have two jobs, and we couldn't understand that because no one in Ireland had more than one job at the time. They'd be working on building sites during the day and be a barman or a cab driver at night.

It was very busy; it was alright to be making money and a good living, but they were working very hard for it.

The same thing is happening in Ireland now. Everyone is working; the housewife is now working, and farmers have jobs on the side so people are working very hard here now.

In New York we would usually stay in the Hotel Manhattan. You wouldn't get any meals there; we'd go to the restaurants nearby. John Kerry O'Donnell, the head man over the GAA in New York, had a restaurant very near the hotel and everyone went in there.

I remember going on the first trip and the Tipperary county secretary, Tommy Barrett stood up on the plane and he gave us a resume of what was going on for the next couple of days, starting off with a banquet in Gaelic Park, the home of New York GAA.

So, we were whisked off to Gaelic Park for this 'banquet' and I noticed some of the boys buttering and eating bread rolls on the table.

I said to Theo English, 'Why don't ye wait for the banquet?'

'This is the banquet,' he replied. 'Get stuck in there or you'll get nothing else.'

It was only a ruse to get us into the pub and drink a bit, and get the crowd to come and see the players that had come over. But, they were great times. Tipperary people out there were very good to us. They used to take us around the city.

The lads were well able to mind themselves and well able to conduct themselves. You'd be told before you go out that you are representing Tipperary and representing your club. Fellas drank lots but it didn't get out of hand.

One of our most famous trips was in 1968. John Kerry O'Donnell was always giving out about the famous Kennedys. Prior to his death, President John F Kennedy had brought in a rule about restricting the number of people coming to America.

That wasn't going down too well with the Irish and the hurling teams out there because they were being weakened. The week we were there in June, John F Kennedy's brother, Bobby was assassinated.

He was lying in state in St Patrick's Cathedral and we all went to pay our respects. There were queues for miles around the different blocks. There was a policeman on duty and Babs Keating started talking to him, and told him we were all from Ireland.

The policeman thought we came over especially for the funeral and he asked us to follow him. We passed the whole queue and walked right in, and saw Bobby Kennedy lying in state. We would have been hours waiting only for that.

We couldn't play the match against New York on the first weekend on account of the funeral. So, we were stuck and had to play the two matches on a Saturday and a Sunday the following weekend, and we still had to win by the aggregate score.

It was hard enough but we managed to pull it off.

I went two or three times to New York. We also went to Chicago and we were in San Francisco in 1971, so we got around.

We met Mayor Richard Daley in Chicago. He was a very famous man; he was supposed to be fairly notorious, a bit of a bulldozer in always getting his own way, but he was mayor for years and his son became mayor after him. We gave him a present of a hurley and I was looking at this fine hurley and I was saying to myself... *What a waste!*

THERE WAS A story told of a Tipperary hurler on the trip who was a farmer. He wanted to buy trousers to wear around the yard at home. There was no tax on clothes in Ireland that time. Anyway, he picked out one that he liked, and he asked the shop assistant, 'How much?'

She said, '10 dollars, plus tax.'

He said, 'I don't want tacks at all... I wear braces.' That was how backward we were.

We also hurled in London a few times, on the famous sod of Wembley in the St Brendan's Cup. I found it a very heavy and very small pitch. There would have been a couple of thousand at those games, but nothing like Gaelic Park where they had huge crowds.

Only for those trips, some of us would never have got outside Ireland.

There was always great regard for hurlers wherever you were in the world, particularly if you were from Tipperary. People would come up to you alright, but I wouldn't be looking for the limelight. I would be dodging away from it as much as I could.

People weren't as critical back then. Although in 1963, when Tipp played Waterford in that Munster final and did everything bar score, Liam Devaney was confronted a few days later. He went somewhere for his dinner, and this fella came down and left his fist on the table and said, 'Ye left it behind ye!'

That would be the size of it; they couldn't believe that the team could be so bad.

By and large, you wouldn't get too much criticism. Though the papers might sew it into you alright.

Hurlers especially were held in high esteem because of the type of game it is. It's an inspiring sort of game. I still get the buzz looking at a game of hurling being played well. I love it.

People respect that you used to stand under the dropping ball, and they remember those things.

You have to be brave. The danger is there all the time, but good hurlers generally didn't get injured. In our time, without helmets, it was much easier to get a cut; you could get cut at any time. Then you had to get stitches after but that was no big deal.

You'd hear great war stories of the toughness of those games, even bordering on savagery but that is over-exaggerated. Fellas would swing their hurleys but once you had your hurl up you were able to protect yourself.

Your hurley was your shield.

Jimmy Doyle was a smashing hurler, but he was also able to mind himself. He was just a handy lad and he'd be getting it hard because he was so dangerous for scoring and the opposition would be getting physical with him. But he could manoeuvre his hurley and flick the ball on one hand and be gone without getting a belt.

We all got our share of them, across the shins or on our arms but by and large I was very lucky, I never had to go off in a game for treatment.

AFTER 1973, TIPPERARY went into a bit of a tailspin and apart from a National League success in 1979, it wasn't until '87 when we tasted major glory again.

We just got on a bad run. We found it hard to put a team together and everyone seemed to be an expert overnight.

Paddy Leahy was gone, and he had been a steadying influence on Tipperary hurling while he was there for almost 20 years. There was never any doubt about who was going to be the manager, only Paddy.

Once he went, the thing was wide open and anyone and everyone could go for jobs, and anyone and everyone got those jobs.

If Tipp were badly beaten, it was time to get new selectors in order to get things turned around. People would write into the local papers and say this is my team for Tipperary, and this is the team that should be playing for Tipperary.

It was criticism all the way from different people. It was a very hard time on everyone. The players got no chance, they didn't know if they were going to be on or not.

◄◄◆▷►

BABS KEATING

Despite all the senior success from 1959 through to '65, the one thing that was absent was success at minor level. Even though there was huge success through the 70s at under-21 level I still contend that minor is more important to a county than under-21. If you are not good enough at 20 or 21 years of age for senior, are you going to be better at 22 or 23?

◄◄◆▷►

I BECAME A selector with the Tipperary seniors from 1983 to '86.

It was a very hard job to motivate players and get them to believe that they could win. The confidence was gone out of Tipperary hurling at the time.

The 1984 Munster final is the one that haunts everyone. It's the one that got away.

We were in dire straits looking for a championship success. We went 10 years without winning a championship game at one stage.

That year, we beat Clare in the Munster semi-final. That win was like a weight lifted off the county as we were into our first Munster final since 1973.

Whatever it was in the 10 years in between, we just couldn't get going. Like any team that falls down, it is hard to get back up again.

It was a gloomy time around Tipperary, and everyone was pessimistic about it. I was never afraid of going in and having a go. I always thought we could do it and in 1984, we knew we had a fairly good team. We knew we were going to play well against Cork, and we were anxious about playing the All-Ireland final in our own county as well, as the Centenary All-Ireland final was going to be played at a redeveloped Semple Stadium.

We played very well against Cork and we were well on top. John McIntyre had a fine game that day at centre-back. However, towards the end we lost our focus, not helped by losing Bobby Ryan to injury, either.

We were four points up with about five minutes to go, and Michael Doyle got a ball and hand-passed it across the square. But the Cork full-back cut it out and cleared it down the field. It went over McIntyre's head and into Séanie O'Leary, who got a shot away at John Sheedy in the goals. He parried it, but the rebound was put into the net by Séanie.

It gave Cork a massive boost and it got them going, and they got another goal from Tony O'Sullivan and went on to win by four points.

It was a game we should have won. However, it was the lack of that real deep belief that we could do this, that was our undoing. There was that little fear coming into the closing stages... *Could we hold on?*

We were just there but we didn't win.

However, there were positive signs and people saw a bit of hope after that, but we didn't have any success in 1985, but in '86 Tony Wall was brought in as coach/trainer and Kilruane were after winning the All-Ireland club final so I was asked back in again. I was initially the coach and Tony the trainer, until the county board requested that Tony do both roles.

It was Tony's first time managing Tipperary. He was ahead of his time with his ideas, but the players found it hard to adjust and see what he wanted them to do. Looking back on it, he was on the right track but he needed more time, and wasn't helped by injuries to key players including Nicky English. We ended up losing 2-10 to 1-11 to Clare in Ennis and our championship summer was over after just one game once again.

We should have been able to do better and that was it for us as the management again.

Tipperary hurling was at a crossroads. There was panic and desperation really. It was unheard of for Tipperary to be down for so long.

It was like people talk now about depression and not being able to see a way out. It was the same in hurling and no one could see a way out.

Everyone thought it would be the next year, but it didn't happen. Once we got the chink of light at all it opened up again and the confidence was back.

Tipperary were trying to get Diarmuid Healy from Offaly, the Kilkenny man who masterminded Offaly's resurgence and managed them to the 1981 All-Ireland title. He turned it down, but eventually they gave the job to my former teammate, Babs Keating and he worked the oracle along with Donie Nealon and Theo English.

We didn't know what to expect from Babs, but he had a big personality. That lifted the players, there's no doubt about that. He got a Supporters Club going.

They raised a good bit of money which allowed for much better treatment of the players. Donie Nealon did most of the coaching; he was an excellent coach.

THE MUNSTER FINAL in Killarney in 1987 will never be forgotten. Tipperary hurled really well but it was still level at full-time. However, I could see the Cork players were wilting, they were very tired going into extra-time. They stayed out on the field while Tipp went into the dressing-room. Tipp walked all over them in extra-time with goals from Michael Doyle and Donie O'Connell.

The whole atmosphere in the county changed after that. Everything was possible once again. The old Tipp swagger was back.

While Galway beat us in the All Ireland semi-final, we were on the right road and the following year we retained the Munster title and reached the All-Ireland final losing to Galway. We finally won the All-Ireland in 1989, beating Antrim in the final, but only after a titanic semi-final win over Galway.

It was amazing how Tipperary were so dominant in the 60s and then for around 15 years in the 70s and through to the 80s, we couldn't win the toss, never mind a match. Once the spell was broken the confidence seeped back in and they went from strength to strength.

The irony is if the county team is struggling, the club championship is generally very good and with Tipperary knocked out early in the championship in the 70s and early 80s, there was only the club championship in the summer, and the North championship invariably provided the county champions.

Moneygall, Roscrea, Lorrha, Kilruane MacDonaghs and Borris-Ileigh were all fine teams while Nenagh Éire Óg were also strong despite not winning anything. There was fine club hurling with good club teams, however, it was hard to pick county players out of them.

Len was fortunate to play against some of the greatest hurlers in the game, and none more so than Kilkenny's Eddie Keher (above); and like Len, many of his opponents also gave back to the game by turning their hand to coaching county teams (below, Richie Bennis of Limerick, on the right, and Gerald McCarthy of Cork).

« CHAPTER 8 »

Where it Begins and Ends

IT WOULD BE easy to look back on my hurling life as achieving success just with Tipperary, but 1965 was also a special year for Kilruane as I captained the club to the North senior title.

Even though I was just 22 years-old, it was sort of the way that the most prominent man at the time was made captain and I had won an All-Ireland with Tipperary in 1964, so I got the job.

It was an honour to be made captain and then to win a championship was terrific altogether. Setting out at the start of the year we didn't think we were going to. We had been waiting since 1959 to win another one.

My brother, Des was on that team and we hadn't won one prior to that since 1944. They were scarce. But 1965 was a fine win; we beat Lorrha in the final and they went on to win it in '66. The late Jim 'Fenor' Ryan was on that Lorrha team and I was marking him, and he was a fine hurler.

I remember with the last ball we got a goal. Des whipped up a clearance that came to Gerry McCarthy 10 yards inside the Lorrha half. He gave it to Tom McLoughney, and he hit it to Séan Williams. He scored the goal that put us into the lead.

However, we didn't win much more with the club until the 70s, when we enjoyed our golden era.

I always loved playing for Kilruane MacDonaghs, and I always wanted to play for the club. I even gave up going places with Tipperary, including to matches over in England, in Wembley.

I didn't go if the club was playing. Munster went to New York one year after winning the Railway Cup and I didn't go. I would rather play for Kilruane MacDonaghs because that is where it all started and where it all would finish.

Nenagh and Borrisokane were where we played most of our big matches. Borrisokane was a great pitch for hurling. Kilruane and Lorrha used to have fierce matches there. I rate Lorrha as the toughest club team I ever played against. They were as hard as nails, but they were straight and honest also. You knew it would be hard before you went out.

They had Johnny and Paddy O'Meara, Phil McIntyre, Paddy Madden, the Lanes, Liam King, the Lack Meara and Liam Moran. They were hardy lads.

Roscrea were a great team as well. They won the first club All-Ireland in 1971 and they were good from there on. Tadhg O'Connor, Francis Loughnane, John Dillon, Owen Killoran and Roger Ryan, each of them spectacular in their own way.

Then came Moneygall in 1975 and '76. They had a lovely team. They won the North and the county title twice. They had the Ryans and the Gleesons.

THAT PERIOD COINCIDED with my transition into coaching with both Kilruane MacDonaghs and Tipperary.

In 1971, the same year I won my third All-Ireland with Tipperary, I coached Kilruane MacDonaghs to the North and county minor hurling titles, and over the course of that decade the club would win six North and four county under-21 titles, which backboned Kilruane's incredible senior success in the late 70s and early 80s, culminating in the All-Ireland club title in 1986.

In all that time, I still found time to work with Tipperary as a coach, as well as a player.

In terms of starting out, the county man was looked on in the parish as knowing more than the rest and that was the way it was.

In 1965, when I was captain of the Kilruane senior team, I did most of the physical training. It followed on from that; we won the North final that year and I was picked to take over the Kilruane minors. As the county man I was given the job.

So, of course, I took it and I thought I could do everything at that age.

Around 1970, I went and did a coaching course at Gormanston College in Meath. Joe Lennon, the famous Down footballer used to run them. Ned Power, the Waterford goalkeeper, my Tipperary teammate, Donie Nealon and Fr Tommy Maher from Kilkenny were some of the coaches as well.

I found it very good. I learned how to deal with people, which is the most important thing as a manager. If you cannot deal with people on a human level, you cannot coach them.

When I was asked to coach by the club, I knew I had to learn something about it, rather than just take over the job, and just start shouting and roaring.

Those are the things that you learned most, how to deal with players and how to bring the best out of them. It is the key.

You cannot put the best into them, you have to get the best out of them.

If you are not on the right wavelength then you will not get the best out of them. I learned that early on, if you could treat them right and by right, I mean the right way. You didn't have to mollycoddle them; just let them know this is the way we are going to play, and this is what we are going to do.

Players love to know what their job is, what their role is, and what the team's aim is. They love to be organised.

When you got on the county senior team, you were nearly expected to know it all. They would just tell you, this fella might be dangerous, maybe keep an eye on this guy or things like that, do not go for goals or go for points, whatever.

I learned early on to organise your team and have them comfortable with what they had to do, because young fellas at under-18, they wouldn't be sure of themselves. None of us are at that age.

The organisation behind a team is very important. If players see that you are serious, being meticulous about being on time and doing the right things, they know then that they are being looked after well, that this fella knows what he is talking about. They will then decide to work hard for their coach or manager.

There is more to it as well. You have to get inside players' heads too. You have to try and work them, and try to get them tuned in when they are with you and get the best out of them.

IN 1972 I coached the Tipperary minors while also playing with the seniors.

The minors were given a trimming by Cork in a Munster semi-final but I wasn't allowed to be with the team as we were playing in the senior match afterwards and I was told by the senior management to focus on that.

The following year the same situation arose again when we got to the Munster final where we defeated Limerick in the minor final, but they got their revenge in the senior final.

It was mad really doing so much when still hurling and having a young family, but people pushed you into these jobs. When it came to hurling, it was hard for me to say no.

I moved on to managing the under-21s in 1974 where we were beaten by Clare in the Munster semi-final. I would stay with the under-21s until 1977, even though we didn't enjoy any success during that time.

◄◄◆►►

PAT MCLOUGHNEY
(TIPPERARY UNDER-21 PANELLIST 1974 AND 2-TIME ALL STAR GOALKEEPER)

I was only after starting to play in goal for the club when I was brought on to the Tipp under-21 panel and I made the team.

We were beaten by Clare in Cashel but I had a good game and was really happy with myself, but Len said to me afterwards, 'You're new to this position… but if you keep working at it there is a place on the bigger stage for you'.

After those few words, I felt I was going to get a chance to play with Tipperary. Every day, after I ate the dinner, I went out and hurled a ball off the wall to try and improve, and do what I needed to do to be a goalkeeper. I did not think of myself as a goalkeeper before then, all I wanted to do was get back out field.

If Len hadn't said that to me, I would have probably put my foot down with the club and said I wanted to play out field.

That year we won the North intermediate title with Shannon Rovers and the following year I was brought on to the Tipp senior panel and would hurl in goal for them for the next seven years.

◄◄◆►►

BACK WITH KILRUANE, when I started off with that group of minors in

1971, you would not have thought they were destined for such greatness. They would have had a bit of success at underage, but it didn't dawn on me that they were a right good group.

I just got into them and worked on them as best I could from what I had learned on coaching courses.

The Williams' were on the team, Tony Shepherd, Billy O'Shea, and Eamon O'Shea came on later. John Quinlan, Dinny and Jim O'Meara, the Cahills, they were all coming along at that stage, too and they developed from there, and got the knack of winning and never lost it.

From winning, players grow in confidence. You learn from the opposition; you learn from everyone.

The more matches you play the more you learn, and they were getting lots of matches because we were staying in the championship longer. If you were beaten in the first round you were gone so it was vital to stay in the championship and try and get as many games into them as you could.

We had a lot of tough battles at under-21 level in which we were lucky enough to come through, and had to stand firm and not fold up.

I HAD BEEN on numerous courses to learn as much as I could about training but I also was influenced by some of the greats of that era and went to see them at sessions.

I went to Dublin to watch Kevin Heffernan training their senior football team in the mid-70s when they were at their peak.

We had to get permission to get in to see them because there was no one allowed into their training sessions, but I knew somebody, and he said it was okay.

I was on my own observing Heffernan doing all these drills and I learned from that, but I didn't get a chance speak to him.

I also went to Kerry to see Mick O'Dwyer training their senior team. I didn't ask anyone, I just walked into Fitzgerald Stadium in Killarney and I had my kids with me.

His style was different to Heffo in how he was talking to the players and how they played the game, that caught my attention.

My kids went down behind the goals and their goalkeeper, Charlie Nelligan was asking who they were, and they gave him their names. He could not believe they came down to see them training.

I did get a chance to speak with O'Dwyer. He wanted me to go in for the meal after training, but I didn't want to impose myself too much.

I was sorry afterwards that I didn't as I would have gotten lots more information. He was a very nice man and very generous with his time. He gave me lots of advice on things.

It would open your eyes on how they do it and maybe you were not so far wrong yourself, but you would learn something anyway.

It might seem strange that it was two football managers who had the greatest impact on me as a coach, but they were two powerful managers no matter what the code.

It was the era of the cult manager.

Kevin Heffernan was the first and then Mick O'Dwyer came along to end Dublin's dominance and begin a great one of their own.

I followed football at that time as I liked the Dubs. I was at the All-Ireland football final in 1974 when they won their first with that team. Heffernan was in charge of them and I got a great kick out of the Dubs supporters, they were very colourful.

I followed Kerry just as eagerly. I went to all the big matches between Kerry and Dublin. I loved seeing great men playing and how they played, how they brought themselves into the game and how they reacted when things went against them. That would be interesting for me.

Some lads would fold if a goal went in and then you have to get into their heads and tell them the match isn't over until the final whistle goes.

In hurling, you can do a lot of scoring in the last couple of minutes.

The big thing for me was understanding that mistakes happen when you are tired, so do not tire. You had to get lads fit enough to last the hour. Do that, and the mistakes will dry up. You might get beaten, but you won't make mistakes. That is fierce important.

I concentrated on that.

If you get a knock in a game, it knocks the hell out of you, so you had to keep the stomach strong. We did a lot of press-ups and sit-ups to strengthen the stomach area of all of our players.

We did press-ups for the shoulders and arms to be powerful for hurling. There were the legs, of course, and there was plenty of running and jumping. I always like to have players running up a bit of an incline, if I could. We did most of that in MacDonagh Park in Cloughjordan; there is a bank there, it was maybe even steeper at that time.

It was short but if you walked down to the bottom of the bank and ran back up 10 or 12 times, you'd know it, let me tell you.

The lads stuck into it well, they were good to train. We never had any bother with them and with that attitude there was always a chance of winning.

◄◄◆►►

EAMON O'SHEA
(KILRUANE MACDONAGHS)

He might have just been the trainer of the team, but he was the man in charge.

At that time, you normally came into training and played a game. I used to go to training early and Len was always in the dressing-room first. He was a busy man, much busier than I was but he would always be there first.

The sense of belief you got from just seeing him was unbelievable. I was only 19 years of age at the time and making my way, but the belief you got from his personality in the dressing-room was huge. He wouldn't be shouting or roaring, but he'd be there and that was enough. That sense of leadership was really critical in the evolution of that team.

◄◄◆►►

IN 1977, I was asked to train the Kilruane senior team despite being still on the team as a player.

We had been beaten in a county final by Roscrea in 1973. We thought we were going to win it. That was a big setback even though it was my first county final.

But in 1977, we really got going.

Winning a county senior football title in 1975 didn't do us any harm either when it came to knowing how to win on the big stage. We had been beaten in the hurling final after a replay by Moneygall the same year, but we managed to progress to the football final also.

I didn't play football but most of the rest of the lads were good at it – the Williams brothers, Tony Sheppard, big Johnny O'Meara too.

They never trained for football though. They trained with the hurlers as the football team was the hurling team, plus one or two extra guys who didn't play hurling. They had their own selectors.

They got to the county final in Nenagh against Loughmore/Castleiney. Everyone thought they would be beaten. Loughmore were good that time. The very first ball and Loughmore had a fella at centrefield, Séan Kearney and he went high to catch this ball and I thought... *Oh my God, is it going to be like this all day!*

But our lads stuck into it. Ozzie Bennett trained us that year for the hurling, and they pulled him in for football after. At half-time, the players were sort of thinking... *We're not doing too bad.*

Ozzie then stood up.

'We're here to win it!' he told them.

He let a few roars and lifted them, and they tore into it in the second-half and they won.

It was a victory when you look back on it now, that was unbelievable. It was an open draw championship at that time, and you could be drawn against Loughmore in the first round or be drawn against someone from the strong football clubs in the West and South divisions of the county. They were drawn against a few good teams on their way to that title, including two of the aristocrats, Clonmel Commercials and Fethard.

In 1977, we got back into the North senior hurling final where we beat Borris-Ileigh by two points but six weeks later who was waiting for us in the county final, only Borris-Ileigh again.

We drew with them in the first match and it went to a replay. The replay was played in a downpour which continued right through the match, but we won 1-5 to 0-5.

It was unbelievable.

You couldn't do any better with the weather that was in it.

◄◄◆►►

EAMON O'SHEA

I would not have been a typical Kilruane hurler and in a sense, I never felt from Len that it mattered. He said to me one day, 'You are there to pick up the pieces'.

I wasn't strong in any sense of the word. Len was able to see a player's strengths and he went with the strengths.

He was a big man for fitness.

We didn't do drills, which took over in the 80s, we just hurled. We hurled the ball on the pitch, almost freestyle hurling which is almost unheard of now. Essentially it was 30 players on the pitch and balls flying everywhere, and balls would be coming at random to you. I enjoyed that because you could engage with the fellas around you.

He has a sense of the pace and rhythm of the game; he wanted us to play in a particular way.

We also really trained hard, we didn't do weights, but he would set up bales of hay or straw on the field and we would be crashing into them.

He never let me do it. I think he thought if I ran into a bale, I was a goner. But he got me to do other stuff, which was unusual.

Len's view was ahead of his time. It wasn't a special exemption, I wasn't as strong as some of the other lads. He wanted me to be able to keep the strength I had for match day. It was small things like that which made him stand out at that time.

He was a hard taskmaster. He was very emotional and passionate in the dressing-room. He was never one to shout at you, but he would let you know you have to work harder.

When I was coming on to the senior team at the age of 19, he was winding down as a player, but he was still hardy. I remember him coming on in a few games at full-forward and to be honest the ground would shake, the decibel levels would go up, and you knew a change was coming, both from the point of view of ourselves but also the opposition. Because he brought that aura and was an embodiment of who we were at that time.

When he came on, we were usually in trouble on the scoreboard.

He came on full-forward one day against Roscrea and my job was to be around him when the ball broke, so I had to do calculations in my head but they were easy to make with Len as he was ferocious in the tackle and if he got the ball he'd still go for goal.

But I also knew if he got the ball, he would find me if I was in the right position.

◄ ◄ ◆ ► ►

IN 1978, WE followed it by doing the same North and county double, this time beating Roscrea in both finals. In the county final, we were trailing by three points at half-time and the management brought me on at full-forward, and we turned it around and won it by a point. That was a big win because Roscrea were very good at the time.

The same year our intermediates also won the county title. When you think about that now, it would nearly be impossible, but we managed to balance it out. We only used 18 players at senior level, with the rest on the intermediate team.

Billy O'Shea and I played senior one day against Borris-Ileigh because we had a few injuries; we needed to spare the intermediate team.

In 1979, we were struggling early in the year but somehow we managed to get ourselves through to the knockout stages where we found our form to beat Borris-Ileigh, Nenagh and Roscrea before accounting for a fine Moneygall side in the North final. Wins over Holycross/Ballycahill and Cappawhite saw Kilruane into the county final and on the cusp of a three in-a-row, with Thurles Sarsfields standing in our way. We produced our best display of the year to win by six points.

However, I didn't play in that game as I had lost my place on the team. But I was still coach of the team and our fitness levels, as well as our high skill levels, were key to our success.

◄◄◆►►

EAMON O'SHEA

It was a relentless kind of thing. He relentlessly drove us on.

Hurling consumed him. That relentlessness comes from the belief you have. I never believed we were going to lose any game. We did lose games and some days we were terrible but at the same time we never had that sense that we were not going to get to our goal. Even when we would lose a game or would play badly and win, Len would not come out and say we were terrible.

We had good players, we had outstanding club players. There weren't many of us that were brilliant, but we had outstanding players for club level and at the same time that belief was really strong that we would keep going.

He would be very thoughtful in the way he coached games. That wasn't a very tactical era, but he did think tactics and positional sense at a time when the game was very standardised. He would have got me to run into different areas to try and take defenders away and things like that.

He played me at centre-forward one day and back in those days the centre-forwards were hardy, strong men, whereas nowadays a centre-forward would drift off a centre-back to get on the ball. So, it was the 1980 county final against Roscrea, and he put me centre-forward on Tadhg O'Connor and I scored 2-1.

Len saw something at that stage of Tadhg's career that he was vulnerable, and it worked by putting an athletic player on him. The only pity was we lost the game as Roscrea denied us the four in-a-row.

◄◄◆►►

WE GOT BACK to the county final in 1980 but Roscrea denied us the four in-a-row by just one point, with Roger Ryan scoring a last-minute goal to deny us a place in history. We were in hard luck not to win it, but we got the three. It was a special time and special team.

We had a few down years then where we failed to get to a North final, which would have guaranteed progression to the county quarter-finals.

We got going again in 1985 and got through to the North final against old rivals Roscrea and won it by a goal. Such was the strength of the clubs in the North that time, a North final usually led to a repeat in the county final and that is how it was, and at half-time Roscrea had our measure but goals from Pat Quinlan and Eamon O'Shea saw us overturn a four point deficit to win by five.

From there we moved on to the Munster Club Championship. We had been in the Munster Championship in 1977, '78 and '79 but we had not done well. The closest we came was in 1979 where we played Blackrock in Cloughjordan in a tremendous game. They had a great team which included Dermot MacCurtin, Tom Cashman and Ray Cummins, and despite being down to 14 men we were still ahead near the end, but conceded two goals to lose by four points.

When we got through to the Munster Championship again in 1985, I said to the players we are going to go for the All-Ireland. I didn't think about it enough the other years but the fact that the finals were now on St Patrick's Day in Croke Park was a big pull.

If you were a country club, you wouldn't think you could win it. We didn't think that way anyway, but we started to take it seriously in 1985. We had a right match with the Waterford champions, Tallow below in Tallow in the Munster semi-final.

Donie Nealon was secretary of the Munster Council at the time and I happened to meet him one day. Tallow had played the Kerry champions in the first round and I asked him what Tallow were like? He said they were a good team, and warned me we'd want to watch ourselves, so I was on guard.

We had a ripper of a match and they led us the whole way through. Jim Williams took a shot near the end and their goalie made a great save and a big cheer went up from the home crowd.

However, in his excitement, the goalie cleared it straight out over the sideline. Seamus Hennessy took the lineball and sent it into the square, and we got a goal off it from Jim Williams to level it.

Gilbert Williams converted a '70' to win it, 1-18 to 1-17. It was in the middle of November, the wrong time of the year for hurling, but it was a right match.

Blackrock of Cork were awaiting us in the Munster final in Limerick. We led them the whole way and towards the end they came at us and earned a draw. They still had a great team with the Cashmans, Frank Cummins and Eamon Donoghue, who hurled for Cork for years.

Everyone said that was our chance gone.

I said to myself it wasn't our chance gone and I drove it into the boys immediately afterwards in the dressing-room.

◄◄◆►►

GILBERT WILLIAMS
(KILRUANE MACDONAGHS)

In the dressing-room after the drawn Munster final against Blackrock, Len gave what most of us would consider his best ever speech.

Everybody was down after Blackrock had got a late equaliser from a soft free for over-carrying. Most thought our chance was gone but Len's words roused the packed dressing-room. It was his finest hour.

◄◄◆►►

WE HAD A meal in O'Meara's Hotel in Nenagh coming home and I told them, 'We have just as much a right to be favourites as any Cork team'.

We only had a week to prepare as the replay was on the following Sunday.

Unusually for myself, I chose to organise a training session on the Saturday morning, the day before the replay. During the week, I rang Shannon Airport and got the weather forecast for the weekend which was giving it very bad for match day. Saturday was bad as well, so I said I would get them used to the conditions.

I brought them down to the field, but they could not understand why I was training them 24 hours before a game. Training was only a puck around but they got wet and their boots were wet and I got them into the dressing-room. 'The first thing you do is to go home and take off your boots, socks and togs and dry them out,' I told them.

'If it is raining tomorrow... we'll be ready.'

I drove it into them as hard as I could and we beat them double scores, 0-12 to 0-6. Blackrock could not believe it. I went into their dressing-room after the match and their manager, Canon Michael O'Brien was stunned.

I will never forget the look on his face.

They could not understand how we beat them. We just tore into them. It was a great victory.

We played Desmonds from London in Cloughjordan in the All-Ireland quarter-final. That was another mucky day in February. We beat them easily enough and then we played Turloughmore from Galway in Nenagh in the semi-final. They were strong hardy boys, but we beat them fairly well too.

It was on to the All-Ireland club final on St Patrick's Day, and Buffers Alley from Wexford. Tony Doran's team, but they had a few more county lads including Mick Butler, Tom Dempsey and Barry Murphy.

It was a great game, but we were a couple of points down coming into the last five minutes.

I had been warned not to go on to the field by the linesman. However, I was getting anxious to rouse the boys for one final push, so I went down the sideline, across behind the goals and up the Hogan Stand side and let a few shouts into them.

I came back around the very same way. I never went in on the field but as I was coming back around the corner-flag on the Cusack Stand side, one of our lads took a shot across the goal and it went wide.

The sliotar landed at my feet and I just picked it up and threw it back to the goalie, so he could not delay looking for the ball.

He gave me a few verbals but when he took the puck-out, he miss-hit it and Gerry Williams got it and fired it back over the bar. Gerry levelled the match before Gilbert Williams converted a '65' for the lead, with Jim Williams sealing a two-point win.

It was a mighty win for the club. You could imagine what it was like. We went by train from Cloughjordan… the team, the supporters, the whole lot. Three trains left Cloughjordan that day. People who were never at an All-Ireland final in Croke Park went because they knew they would get in and didn't have to have a ticket, just pay in at the game.

Old people I knew were there and they cried. They couldn't believe that our team had won in this big setting in Croke Park.

It was terrific.

One of our sweetest wins came in the 1987 North final against Lorrha. We were not given much chance, but the lads produced a performance of savage intensity to win by eight points. While we did not go on to win the county title, that North title was sweeter than them all.

◄◄◆►►

GILBERT WILLIAMS

To say the least, we were in a bit of disarray at training the Tuesday night before the North final. To make up the numbers Len played in the bit of a match but suffered a broken nose. He continued playing in the match despite the injury.

◄◄◆►►

THAT INJURY WAS a funny one as I rarely suffered a major injury in my hurling career, bar a broken wrist when I was under-21.

Even though I was coming towards the end of my playing days and was training the senior team, I still loved stepping in and playing in a training match if we were short numbers.

That night in 1987, I got a bad blow of the ball into my face which led to three bones broken under my eye, as well as a broken nose.

I had to go to hospital and the doctor said I would need an operation to straighten the nose. I had the operation in Limerick and when the procedure was finished the nose was still crooked and the surgeon said he couldn't do any more to it.

I wasn't put out by it. I was well able to breathe normally and had no problem going around with a crooked nose for the rest of my life.

I had suckler cows at home on the farm and sometime later, I was trying to put a second calf on a cow, not her own calf, and she was very contrary about it. I had her penned up in the yard between gates, trying to push the calf in under her but the cow wasn't having any of it and was kicking back and being awkward.

She then gave the gate a fair kick and it swung back, and hit my nose a right belt.

I said to myself… *My nose is in bits again.*

I went into the house to have a look in the mirror to see the damage and wasn't the nose straight as an arrow again, the cow's belt from the gate did the job the surgeon couldn't.

THAT KILRUANE TEAM from 1977 to '86 were a super group. Some lads would be more leaders than others. Some would be quiet and just play their game and that was it.

The Cahills were very strong, Dinny in particular. Dinny O'Meara and Jim O'Meara were rock solid. The Williams', Gerry, Paddy, Jim, and Gilbert were sound men. You could depend on them and they would know when to lift it a bit if things was going wrong. They were great that way, you could rely on them.

I didn't say much from the sideline, just a few shouts to get them going if they needed that. I do not like telling players too much of what to do with the ball. They are doing that with young lads now and they are destroying them. When you have the ball in your hand the last thing you want to hear is someone roaring at you to do this with it or that with it.

That knocks your brain out.

◄◄◆►►

EAMON O'SHEA

He was our spiritual leader.

He was leading us in a different way than the current managers. It is very different now being a manager than it was then. You didn't do much managing back then; it was much easier. You were trained on the nights you were given; you came in and did your work. There wasn't the same level of people management, but he led everything we did.

Back then the concept of a trainer, was someone in the old-fashioned sense. It was more than that with Len. It was leading by example. When you went to training – and it is a sign of someone who leads – your eyes went to him straight away.

You gravitated towards him. His mood was always towards the team and bringing them along. Nowadays there is a lot more one-to-one stuff. Back then, you had to bring a collective with you and he was brilliant at that.

He almost gave you a reason to perform. He would not necessarily say it to you directly, it was almost a casual way. He was also more nuanced than that.

When we played with Kilruane, there were a lot of great leaders on that team, the likes of Dinny Cahill, the Williams', my own brother, Billy, but Len managed to bring people together and that was a big thing.

He would be hard on you in one sense as well. In 1985 when we won the county final against Roscrea, I played really well and scored 1-4, which was unusual for me. We were chatting after the game and Len complimented me on a great point I scored.

I asked him which one? 'The point where you held off your man and won the ball', he said. Len was saying to me, you had to work hard for that one, whereas with the others I didn't have to. He was challenging us all the time to be better. That never left me, that ability to stay hungry and stay focused.

You do not see special times when they are actually happening, you can only see them retrospectively. When we look back, that was something else to sustain that level of performance for four years first of all from 1977 to '80, then drop back and then come back again in 1985 to win a county, Munster and All-Ireland titles.

If you were to tell me in 1982, I was going to win an All-Ireland Club Championship I would not have believed you. Even when we suffered the inevitable decline after 1980 the heart was still beating. It might not have been beating as strong as in the late 70s but it grew strong again, and we got a bit of luck in 1985. I don't think we would have won in 1985 without the soreness of not winning anything for the previous five years, it created that hunger.

1985 WASN'T JUST ABOUT the senior team going on to win the All-Ireland. The junior team also won the county title and I captained the team at the age of 41, along with Michael McGrath, when we beat Cappawhite.

Not only was I playing for the Kilruane juniors and training the Kilruane seniors, I was also training Shannon Rovers intermediates as well.

I don't know how it came about but the junior and intermediate North finals were played in Nenagh on the same day and I was playing in the junior final against Toomevara and the Rovers were in the intermediate final against Portroe.

We had a right match with Toomevara. They were beating us by 12 points at one stage, but we fought back, and a late Dan Darcy goal earned us the win.

I didn't even wait for the cup presentation and I went straight into the dressing-room with my togs on and gave the Rovers boys a bit of a gee-up before they went out and they won as well.

We then got to the county final in junior 'A'. There was one lad on the Kilruane team, Peter Moyles. He was a cross-country runner and was fit as a fiddle.

He didn't do that much hurling, but he was a very honest player.

I said to him one day, 'Peter you're going well'.

Len, he says, 'I have one problem… when I get the ball, I don't know what to do with it'.

I nearly dropped to the ground as I didn't think anyone would think like that.

'I'll tell you what to do,' I said to him. 'The minute you get the ball, hit it into me.' I was full-forward.

It then dawned on me that maybe some fellas don't know what to do with the ball. You might want them to do this or do that, but the general thing is you hit it near the goal. I made it simple for him and said, 'Hit it straight to me'.

We went on to the county final against Cappawhite. That was the time things were going badly for Tipperary. Everyone was looking for any sign of some new talent coming.

I was playing full-forward and we beat them fairly well and I got 1-5, as I was on the frees.

One auld lad was at the match and next thing another lad came in beside him for the second match which was the intermediate final.

He asked your man if there was any sign of anyone promising on these teams for the county? 'No,' came the reply. 'But there is one lad there, number 14 for

Kilruane… he isn't too bad.'

I was 41 at the time.

I got a great kick out of it when I heard that story.

I got great satisfaction out of winning that championship too as they were grand lads that had not won much up along.

I STAYED HURLING for another few years but as much joy I get out of coaching, it is not the same as playing.

I miss playing like I'd miss one of my hands.

It was unbelievable. I just could not come to terms with it, that I could not hurl anymore.

I could hurl but I was not good enough for a team.

I could still hit the ball fairly well until I was 70.

You think you could still do it.

Then my own kids were growing up and I was pucking with them in the yard and we had great fun. Ciara was seriously good, she used to be boring a sponge ball at me and I was able to catch it and it would drive her mad.

A year or two later, she was able to drive the ball through me as I was getting slower and she was getting stronger.

Coaching is not the same; it is the next best thing to playing. You only have those few years and you have to make the most of them.

I feel I did make the most of it.

I tried my living best anyway.

Len quickly proved his ability as a coach with Kilruane and Tipperary underage teams, and also had a major influence as a manager on men who would lead the Premier County to All-Irelands in the future, like Eamon O'Shea and Liam Sheedy (below).

« CHAPTER 9 »

Going the Extra Mile

EVEN THOUGH I was training the Kilruane MacDonaghs seniors and still hurling with the junior team, my love of hurling was all consuming and it was hard to say no when other clubs approached me to get involved.

My first job outside of Kilruane was with Moycarkey/Borris in 1982.

Paddy 'Sweeper' Ryan was supposed to have said when I went to Moycarkey/Borris… 'A country man for a country team'… and for me to get that vote of confidence from such an esteemed hurling man was huge.

I only joined Moycarkey late in the '82 campaign as I never trained another team while Kilruane were in the championship and in that year, Roscrea knocked us out at the North semi-final stage.

I never went looking for any managerial job. Even with Clare and Tipperary, I never applied for jobs. I was asked to do them. Moycarkey/Borris hadn't won anything for 42 years and were mad for some success.

◄◄◆▷►

LIAM HENNESSY
(MOYCARKEY/BORRIS CHAIRMAN 1982)

We won the Mid championship in 1981 but were beaten by Borris-Ileigh in the county semi-final so we weren't far away. In 1982, we won the Mid final again, and after that we felt we needed somebody to give us an extra shove on.

Len Gaynor's name was mentioned as Kilruane has been knocked out of the North championship at that stage. Gussie Ryan would have been involved with Len on a county minor selection committee in the 70s and would have been friendly with him, so the club agreed for Gus to make contact with Len and he agreed to come on board, and the rest is history.

Our lads improved as the year went on and won a county final, after a replay over Roscrea.

It was Len who made the difference. We were doing a lot right but getting to the county semi-finals in the previous years, the standard rose noticeably, particularly playing the North clubs who were powerhouses in the 70s and 80s. They were at a different level. I remember the 1980 county final between Kilruane and Roscrea, it was a top-class game and we'd be saying to ourselves… Could we ever reach that standard?

Len knew what it took to reach that standard and was able to push our lads to get the best out of them. They were a good skilful group anyway, but they needed to be pushed that little bit more.

◄◄◆►►

I FOUND MOYCARKEY very strong hurlers and very strong-minded people. There was a very genuine toughness about them in hurling.

I wanted to try and give them self-belief as well.

We had great times there. I really enjoyed it. It was a long drag down… 32 miles, three times a week after work, but I really enjoyed it.

Eileen gave me great support all the way through. She looked after things at home when I was gone. I used to take the kids with me to training an awful lot once they were big enough to go. They'd hurl away behind the goals, while I'd be with the team.

It broadened their outlook a little bit too, meeting different people. There would be old lads on the sideline, and they'd be watching training and they'd give my lads a few bob, and we'd call into the first shop going home and spend it. It was a great bonding time with them. They really enjoyed it too.

◄◄◆►►

CIARA GAYNOR
(5-TIME ALL-IRELAND SENIOR CAMOGIE WINNER)

He was always going training and we always wanted to go with him or when there was a match on.

With him everything centred around hurling which was lovely, and he would bring us to training, whether it was Kilruane, Shannon Rovers or Clonoulty/Rossmore. Or Clare or Tipperary.

I used to love hearing him talk to the teams. I remember the games and the importance of them and the training, and the excitement in the build-up.

If we did anything wrong at home our punishment was we weren't allowed go training with him; that's how much we enjoyed going with him. We used to go to Clare two or three nights a week, the same with the Tipp sessions, as well as the club.

Joe Hayes stood for me for my Confirmation. Dad would have been with Clonoulty in 1989 and I made my Confirmation a year later, and I asked Joe.

They didn't bat an eye-lid when I told them that Joe was going to sponsor me, but they loved Joe as well and they were happy to see him there on the day. It was probably another excuse as well for dad to talk hurling for the day.

◄◄◆►►

THERE WEREN'T TOO many county men in Moycarkey at the time, bar Jack Bergin. John McCormack was centre-forward, while the talented John Flanagan was still going strong.

We won the county final in 1982. We drew with Roscrea the first day and beat them in a replay.

Like Tipperary at the time, Moycarkey/Borris were lacking a bit of confidence. Roscrea were going very well in the first-half, but we were only trailing by a point. We went into the dressing-room at half-time and the players were down.

Suddenly, someone stood up and let out a few shouts, but I let a roar at him to sit down and wait. They were going out to be slaughtered if they didn't focus.

I said, 'This match isn't over and ye can do a lot better than that.' I gave them a good talking to, and they went out to hurl like devils in the second-half and it finished in a draw with Francis Loughnane earning a replay for Roscrea.

In the replay, the experience of the drawn game stood to us and we roared home to a seven-point victory. It was the first of two county titles in three years for Moycarkey/Borris, although I wasn't with them for their 1984 success.

They went on to win the Munster Club Championship, beating Patrickswell in the final but were defeated in the All-Ireland semi-final by Loughgiel Shamrocks of Antrim who went on to win the title.

I went back to Kilruane in 1983 and '84 when I was also involved with the Tipperary senior hurlers.

In 1985, I was approached by Shannon Rovers to come on board with their intermediate team. I didn't know how good or how bad they were at the time.

They were a reasonable team, but hadn't had any success, not a lot since the days of Jim and Ailbe Burke, who were tremendous hurlers.

The journey of 10 miles was also very manageable.

◂◂◆▸▸

PAT MCLOUGHNEY
(SHANNON ROVERS)

We had a players' meeting that winter. We had gone two years without doing much. John Tierney got on to Len Gaynor and asked him would he come in and coach us, and he said he would.

We were all brought to a meeting in Ballinderry hall, which was an unusual thing to do in the 80s. We never had such a crowd of players at the meeting when they heard Len Gaynor was going to be there.

His training was tough, but he never did any of the training from the sideline, he was in with the lads running around the field, doing the sprints, everything. He wouldn't expect anyone to do something he couldn't do himself.

I didn't think there was any big science to it. He instilled this belief that everything you did was the right thing and you were going to be the better for it. He had you fairly convinced going out the day of a match that you were going to win.

◂◂◆▸▸

YOU HAD TO be a psychologist in hurling that time.

It all comes through the brain anyway. If the heads aren't right, you won't play right. So, you have to look on it that way; how are you going to improve yourself and how can you improve yourself?

When you go from junior up to senior or from senior club to the county, the game gets faster.

The big thing to make your game faster is to be better than your opponents, so how do you do it?

Some people think it's running, that you had to be faster running to the ball but it's not actually that at all. You can be faster to the ball but if you are not able to rise it properly, your opponent will catch up on you.

The big thing is moving the ball and controlling the ball quickly, rather than taking two or three hops on the hurley you catch it, then you're in control and can look around and see where you can hit, and what you can do with it.

To get those few fine points right is the big thing, and fellas have to really buy into that and concentrate on that.

You also had to have the heads right and tuned in. I never went for this thing of laying down the law, be it no more drink or no more smoking or no more dances. Or keep away from the girlfriend or whatever.

It was pointless laying down those sorts of laws because someone is going to break them and what are you going to do then? If you want to stick to your word, you have to drop that player and if you're dropping him you are cutting off your own nose as you are short a player then. And the next player that is replacing him probably won't be as good.

So, it's better to get them to realise it themselves; that you can't burn the candle at both ends and play good hurling as well.

Something had to give, and I would suggest if you were drinking four pints a night to cut it back to two. I wouldn't say to cut it out fully because they might be better off having the couple of pints before a game, it would relax some fellas.

It didn't do Johnny Pilkington any harm any night before he hurled for Offaly.

What I found was having a pint is okay, even having three or four pints was okay, but it was the amount of time you're sitting or standing having those pints and fellas blowing into you about how you should do this and how you should do that. That could be a problem alright!

When you get into that atmosphere, all your sensibilities go out the window as far as I'm concerned. You are wasting time and hearing the wrong words.

THAT WAS ONE of the big things with a club like Shannon Rovers, and in all my years of coaching they were the hardest team I had to motivate. There was good craic amongst them, but they wouldn't get over-excited about their hurling. They liked their hurling, but they'd be laughing and joking about something else as well.

When I got them going, they were a willing bunch and turned into a fine team.

In 1985, we got to the North final against Portroe, which was the second game of a double-header in Nenagh – with the junior 'A' final I was playing in with Kilruane – so I wasn't able to be with the Rovers team for much time before the game.

◂◂◆▸▸

PAT MCLOUGHNEY

Kilruane were well behind at half-time but started to come back, playing with the wind in the second-half.

We were waiting in the dressing-room and looking out through the small windows checking the scoreboard and Kilruane were coming back, and they got a late goal to win it.

When the final whistle sounded, we could see Len running the whole way from the pitch to the dressing-room and a cheer went up in our room when he came in. From that moment, we were never going to lose that North final because his presence in the room meant so much to everybody.

◂◂◆▸▸

WE GOT AS far as the county semi-final but were beaten by Moycarkey/Borris.

With Kilruane MacDonaghs' second team promoted to intermediate off the back of winning the junior 'A' title the year before, I hadn't planned on going back to Shannon Rovers as we were in the same grade and could have been hurling against one another, but when Kilruane exited the championship I returned to Shannon Rovers.

There were some fine players on the team, including Jim McLoughney who scored a point from a line-ball to draw the North semi-final against Portroe and we went on and won the replay in extra time.

We defeated Nenagh Éire Óg in the North final and moved on to the county championship and eventually reached the county final where we would play Clonmore.

◄ ◄ ◆ ▷ ►

PAT MCLOUGHNEY

On the week of the county semi-final, we were due to have training on the Tuesday evening. I was at the cattle mart in Nenagh. There was a big sale on and I knew at six o'clock that I wasn't going to make training as the cattle wouldn't be sold by then.

I went into the mart office and rang Len, and I said to him that I wouldn't make training as the cattle wouldn't be sold before eight o'clock.

'That's not good enough for me', said Len. 'Anyone can sell the cattle... but you have to train. You are one of the senior members of the team... you have to be there.'

So I had to think.

I went home and collected my father and brought him into the mart to sell the cattle, and I went back to training in Ballinderry.

When I was driving back to Nenagh after training to collect my father at the mart, I knew going home I was after doing something a little bit extra that I would have never done before.

I don't think anyone only Len Gaynor would have got me to do it. He didn't offend me, he just said you have to be there Pat, it's a county semi-final, it would look bad if you are not there.

When I got there, everyone was there, there were lads after coming from Cork, Dublin, and other places so I knew he was after getting me to do the right thing.

It was those aspects that made Len stand out from any other coach I ever played for.

After winning that county semi-final, Len came into the dressing-room afterwards. 'There will be no training Tuesday night!' he announced.

We didn't know why but he then said anyone working away from home was to take a day or a half day off work on Wednesday, and be in Ballinderry for training at three o'clock in the afternoon.

Everyone was wondering how are we going to do this?

I arrived there at half past two and nearly everyone was in the dressing-room before me.

I remember people passing the field and seeing us training in the middle of the day and they blew their horns. It was a kind of recognition from the people of the parish that we were doing something special to try and win. It was a huge thing for us at the time.

There was nothing spared that day.

It wasn't a puck around; it was a full-blown training session and we went on to win the final against Clonmore the following weekend.

When I was managing Portroe in 1990, and when we got to a county final, I did the very same with them by calling a midweek afternoon training session and the Portroe lads will always tell me that that was the day we won the county final. Because you knew you had done something special during the week.

It was a brilliant two years. He couldn't come with us in 1987 as we were senior, and he was training Kilruane seniors. However, in 1987 and '88 at senior level we were still a way better team than we were at intermediate level because we had been educated by Len. His impact was huge on us.

◄ ◄ ◆ ▷ ►

I WAS COMING out of the National Ploughing Championships in Carlow in 1989 and a man by the name of Owen Ryan 'Rody' came over to me and asked me would I come and train the Clonoulty/Rossmore seniors.

I told him I didn't know.

'Ye are a long way away… nearly 30 miles,' I told him.

'We have a good auld team,' he says. 'What we need is for someone to lift them.' And, of course, he talked me into it.

They were more or less the same as us in Kilruane in terms of population and that. They had just won the West final for the first time since 1951 so they weren't going too bad.

Kilruane were out of the championship so I went down to them, and I got them all together on the first night and I gave them a good talking to. I said everyone gets a chance to win something, but you have to take the chance when it comes. I talked to them very straight and told them what I expected from them. And they gave it their all, they trained like devils and hurled like devils.

They had a great team... John Kennedy, Joe Hayes and Declan Ryan, who won All-Ireland senior medals with Tipperary that year.

They also had Peter Hayes, Kevin Ryan at centre-back and Cecil Ryan was full-back. Dan Quirke was a young forward and would score a hat-trick that year for Tipp under-21s in the All-Ireland final against Offaly, with Declan Ryan captaining that team. Andrew Fryday was also a terrific goalie, so there was plenty of talent there.

There was great character in the team with great ability as well.

They had defeated Cappawhite in the West final before I got involved. We beat Loughmore/Castleiney in the county quarter-final and Toomevara in the semi-final, setting up a final against Holycross/Ballycahill, who would be their neighbours even though they play in different divisions with only the river Clodiagh dividing the parishes.

The first-half was a real dour affair where defences ruled, and we led 0-8 to 0-5 at half-time.

A Peter Hayes goal early in the second-half put us in a strong position leading by six points but Holycross managed to get it back to a point. In the closing stages a '65' from John Kennedy sealed a 1-11 to 1-9 win, and Clonoulty/Rossmore's first county senior title in 101 years.

◄ ◄ ◆ ► ►

DECLAN RYAN
(CLONOULTY/ROSSMORE AND TIPPERARY)

Len came from a successful club, which we weren't at the time relative to where we are today. He brought a new impetus to us. He always brought great energy to training and it transferred on to the field in games.

He gave us confidence to play at a level we weren't used to at senior club level at that time. He spoke about winning the county championship when we won the West final. The fact we had won a West final was a big achievement in itself at the time.

We had a particularly good team with seasoned campaigners such as John Kennedy, Joe Hayes, who had won a senior All-Ireland that year, as well as Dan Quirke.

It was more leadership Len gave us.

It wasn't a mental blockage because some of the lads had been successful at underage level with Tipp, so they knew what winning was about, but it was a fact that it was new to the club. While we had good people over us, getting to the county series was something that needed an extra bit of leadership.

The training was particularly good for club level. We really enjoyed it. He brought a few new things; he was all into ball striking. Physical fitness wasn't the main priority as we had been through that earlier in the year and we were now into the county quarter-final stage when Len came in with us.

However, he did bring the hay bales with him to training and he fired them at us, but we were a bit fitter back then than now thank God.

He knew what we were heading into, as he had been there with Kilruane and Moycarkey, as well as with Tipperary as a player. He brought a bit of confidence and we played a more direct style of hurling under his guidance.

His passion for the game! If you cut him, he would bleed ash, that's the way he is. He is just chiselled in the GAA. That came through in his pre-match talk of what he expected from each player on the field.

He also made sure you were in the right frame of mind and you were prepared to give what was required.

He got on very well with the club. I remember his kids at the time, they weren't small, but they used to be down in the hurling field with us.

He brought a great enthusiasm and there was always great excitement when training was going on.

◄ ◄ ◆ ▷ ►

IF I WASN'T busy enough in 1989 after training Kilruane MacDonaghs seniors and then taking up with Clonoulty/Rossmore, I also got involved with Newport intermediate team.

I was approached by their manager, Denis Floyd to come on board after their trainer had an accident after the North semi-final. Training two teams at the same time was logistically difficult but I knew Newport well having come up against them when I trained Shannon Rovers.

◄ ◄ ◆ ▷ ►

DENIS FLOYD
(NEWPORT MANAGER)

1989 was the third year in-a-row we were in the North final. We were beaten by Silvermines in 1987 but won it in '88 beating Templederry. However, we were beaten in the county semi-final.

We were anxious to make the breakthrough and make the step forward to senior level.

Tony Hassett was our trainer, and a good one at that, but he had an accident after the North semi-final against Silvermines.

We felt we needed a little extra hurling-wise, so Len was always a good friend of the club. He would often come to help out with an odd training session… so we called on him.

I would have known him through the North board when he was the North board representative on the county board. I gave him a phone call and he said yes… it was as simple as that. He was always very obliging, which was the one thing I found about Len, whether it was to take a training session, present medals… anything at all.

We beat Portroe in the North final. It was a good game of hurling, there were three goals scored early on and I remember Len saying at half-time, 'This is senior hurling boys'.

Len was always one for direct hurling, that was his style. He didn't want players delaying too much on the ball. Keep the ball moving was his motto.

He was coach of the team but as management we would take a lot of what he would have to say on board in terms of making changes during a game. Fellas had good time for him. He was a great man to give a talk before a match, he would really rile fellas up.

We went on to hammer Fethard in the county semi-final, and beat Thurles Sarsfields in the county final.

It was a huge boost to the club to get back up to senior and much of the team that won the North senior title in 1996 were still there from that '89 intermediate team such as Ger Bradley and Dinny Ryan, who played under-21 for Tipperary that year.

◄ ◄ ◆ ► ►

I ALSO DID a stint with the Templederry Kenyons intermediates in 1991 but we were beaten in the North semi-final, while in 1992 I was asked to get involved with the Moneygall under-21 hurlers.

Former GAA president and Moneygall club stalwart, Séamus Ó Riain arrived at the house with a few lads wondering if I would go and help them out. They knew they had a good team. They were well organised. They didn't really need me; they would have won it anyway, but I got involved.

Our toughest match was against Roscrea in Borrisokane in the North final. Roscrea were winning the whole way through the grades and were strong favourites.

Our goalkeeper, Philip Quinlan, who was only a minor, was a great out-field player. We were six points down with five minutes to play and we had sort of said before the match that if we were stuck we'd bring him out field. And he scored a last second goal to earn a replay which we won and went on to beat Cashel King Cormacs in the county final.

They had a cracking young team at the time, including the likes of John Doughan and Paudie Whyte, who were unfortunate when they progressed to senior level to come across the Toomevara team in their prime and because of that they didn't get the success their talent and work ethic deserved.

No matter what team I was involved with, I always got great satisfaction when I saw lads improve, give their living best and enjoy their hurling. That for me is everything. It is sad to see lads that have ability and don't ever tap into it fully, or express themselves fully and get the best out of themselves.

They are in every club; fellas so good, but wouldn't give the last vital bit. They didn't know how to I suppose. Management is about getting into the heads of players and getting them to understand what it takes to win, and what they need to do to achieve it, and what they need to ask themselves to get the best out of themselves.

That's more important than hurling really.

Everybody can play hurling but how do you get that last bit more out of yourself than your opponent, that's the big thing.

Ciara, Len and Eileen (below) enjoy a moment of triumph in Croke Park.

His career as a coach and manager took Len to many other teams throughout Tipperary, but nobody benefitted more from his expert tutelage than his own children, especially Ciara. Here she prepares for one of Tipperary's All-Ireland senior camogie victories (above) and in action against Cork.

« CHAPTER 10 »

Raising the Banner

BISHOP WILLIE WALSH
(CLARE SELECTOR 1991, '92 AND '94)

Clare hurling was at a very low ebb. We had been beaten by Kerry in a play-off for a trip to London at the end of the 1990 league; that was how low we were.

GER LOUGHNANE
(CLARE SELECTOR 1992 AND '94, MANAGER 1995-2000)

When you look at the history of Clare hurling, there is a pattern where in every decade they produced a team that was capable of making a breakthrough in Munster.

In the 30s they won a Munster Championship, and, in the 40s, they won an Oireachtas competition and there was great talk of that team. In the 50s there was the famous 1955 Munster final they lost to Limerick after beating Tipperary and Cork, the two best teams in the country at the time.

In the 60s they had a really good team which included Jimmy Smith, but they came up against a very good Tipperary team.

In the 70s there were three Munster final defeats and then in the 80s there were two more Munster finals losses.

The pattern after being beaten in those Munster finals was always to go into a downward spiral afterwards. Clare got to a Munster final in 1986 and had the best chance ever of beating Cork in Killarney, because Cork were desperately poor on the day, unusually poor for them.

Clare didn't win and the following year they drew with the emerging Tipperary team of English and Fox and all those great players in the Munster semi-final in Killarney but in the replay Clare got the mother and father of a beating from Tipperary and that led to another free-fall after that.

It didn't matter who was in charge of the team; it was no reflection on Séan Hehir, who took over then and subsequently Tony Kelly. Spirits were down and a lot of players retired after that, including myself.

There was a real shortage of quality players in Clare but the only bright thing on the horizon was Clare got to the All-Ireland minor final in 1989 where they were beaten by Offaly, but there were players of great promise in the likes of Davy Fitzgerald and Jamesie O'Connor.

Also, St Flannan's and the Comprehensive School in Shannon played in a Harty Cup final the same year so there was talent coming.

When Len arrived in 1990, the thing was at a desperately low ebb. Clare had not only been beaten the previous four years, they had suffered some hammerings. It was as low as I ever remember it in my time, not only in terms of morale but also in terms of quality players.

To that end, he was the right man at the right time for that group of players, as Len is such an optimist. There was an uplifting quality to him in everything he did, and he was a man that found the right words for the right occasion. He had great ability that way. People could see that he brought that Tipperary attitude with him.

That was both a strength and a weakness.

It was a strength in that he exuded confidence and optimism. He instilled belief into players… 'Why haven't you the right to win a Munster Championship?'

'Why isn't it your right to be a winner the same as any other county?'

The reason it also was a weakness was, he came from a totally different culture in Tipperary where there was a culture of winning.

There were two stories that always lingered in my mind when I joined him in 1992 that he told, that showed the challenge he faced when he came to Clare. The first was, Tipperary were training for an All-Ireland final in the 60s in Thurles and at the end of this training session they were to do three laps of the field. They did one lap of the field and coming to the end of it John Doyle said, 'That's enough lads… we'll go into the dressing-room'. And they did.

They ignored the trainer and togged in, and they still won the All-Ireland… so you know what you have when you can do that.

The second story was Tipperary were playing Kilkenny in an Oireachtas final and were eight points down at half-time. They went into the dressing-room and talked away the same as if it was a club match and then just before they went back out Theo English said, 'Come on lads… let's go out and beat these fellas'. And they did.

Len came from a completely different mentality from what they had in Clare, where they were only used to disappointment. The hardest thing when you are going from a county whose culture you are so familiar with into another county is to try and decipher what is the mentality in that county.

What is the motivation of players and what way do they think about the game?

Len came with that mentality of, 'Why can't we win?', which is great for players to hear and it did lift the players, but in order to get those players to the standard Tipp were – because he didn't have the same quality of players – your preparation had to be at a different level than in Tipperary.

Even as it was, Len couldn't understand how defeatist the Clare mentality was. I'd say to this day he still doesn't understand how Clare people, when they get to finals because of the collateral damage for all the defeats down through the years, how that mentality creeps in there and just paralyses them in finals.

Len couldn't be expected to understand that, and he would never understand that as he never experienced that with the teams he played on.

◄ ◄ ◆ ▷ ►

IN THE AUTUMN of 1990, I got a phone call from Brendan Vaughan, chairman of Clare County Board and he asked me would I become their senior hurling manager.

Initially I said I wouldn't, but he was persistent, and he asked could we meet at least first, so I agreed, and we met at the Greenhills Hotel in Limerick.

He was a very nice man and ultimately convincing. I had been in school in St Flannan's in Ennis for five years, so I had a relationship with Clare, and I knew a bit about them and what made them tick. I decided I would go and give a bit back, while also testing myself in the senior county game.

◄ ◄ ◆ ▷ ►

BISHOP WILLIE WALSH

The problem then was to get selectors because literally at the time no one wanted to get involved. Brendan Vaughan approached me, and I declined as I was too busy, I was effectively parish priest of Ennis at the time. I was also involved with my own club, Éire Óg Ennis and had a number of other irons in the fire.

Brendan Vaughan couldn't find selectors and he came back to me in desperation and he said it would be terrible if we brought Len Gaynor all the way from Tipperary but had no selectors for him. Then I agreed to go in and we managed to get former manager, Tony Kelly on board as well.

I would have known all the underage players in the county, as well as most of the senior players because I would have been involved with teams in St Flannan's over the years as well as the Clare minors and under-21s.

◄◄◆►►

WHEN I ACCEPTED the job, I knew what I wanted to do.

The first thing was to build a panel. It wasn't easy, Clare were at a low ebb and some players didn't want to join the panel. However, the big thing was whoever we did get to commit were going to be serious about it.

When we finally confirmed a panel, a meeting was called before the first training session. It was in the middle of winter and I remember the first session was to take place in Crusheen. I looked up how to get to Crusheen and when I got to the hurling field, it was locked up with not a sinner in sight.

What I didn't know was there was another pitch belonging to the county board outside the town and that's where they were assembling, so it was a bad start on my behalf.

Eventually, I found it and we started training and I had a good talk with them and told them what I expected of them.

Anthony Daly, Davy Fitzgerald, Brian Lohan, Fergie Tuohy, Ger 'Sparrow' O'Loughlin were there. Jamesie O'Connor came along later, with Séanie McMahon in 1994.

◄◄◆►►

ANTHONY DALY
(CLARE CAPTAIN 1992-1999)

The passion he brought was what I was gasping for.

I had been there for two years and could see no hope at all but suddenly, this guy came along and started talking the things you wanted to hear.

I wasn't enjoying college to be honest but when February came around I was thinking of heading over to my brother in England for a while, but I managed to get a job in a bank and ended up with a good manager in Martin Coffey from Nenagh. He used to follow the hurling, was a member with St Joseph's Doora-Barefield and often he used to say to me, 'Do you know who would be the right man for you... it would be Len Gaynor'.

I went into work one morning and Martin had the papers inside and said, 'Now, what did I tell you. I was prophetic... look at your new manager!' I was delighted.

A couple of weeks later I got to hear him giving his first speech to us and straight away he started talking about winning Munster Championships and that is what I wanted to hear.

It was a breath of fresh air.

◄◄◆▷▶

I DIDN'T KNOW what to expect starting off. I couldn't see what they were to become the first day I spoke to them. I knew they were listening to me, but I didn't know how deep they were taking it in.

It took a tragedy for me to learn a little bit more about them. John Moroney was killed in a car crash in late 1993. He had been on the panel for a good few years before that. His removal was on in Ennis and we all went to it. I remember the night; it was milling rain. The boys lined up outside in the rain waiting to give him a guard of honour.

I said to myself... *There's something about these lads.*

I could see it in them that night. It struck me that they were loyal to him and were prepared to get drenched to see him off.

I could see the eagerness in the training as well, they were anxious to improve and get better. The barrier was there from not having success.

Fellas weren't sure.

◄◄◆▷▶

ANTHONY DALY

There were a few nights in Crusheen where we did the hard slogging over the years. He had us sprinting and half-way across the field you'd be met by a bale of hay flung by a fella from the other side. Manys a night I came from training and the face destroyed from the hay! It was all done to harden you.

Everything he did was done with an intensity. You can have trainers with the best drills ever but if you don't carry them out with a bit of passion, it's not much good.

Len really worked on that and brought that intensity to our training; you couldn't bring it into the matches without bringing it into training.

We were very inconsistent at the time, but we were getting there. The shit was being beaten out of us but, slowly but surely, the bigger counties were being taken on in league games. A draw here or a great win against Waterford down in Dungarvan. Little milestones along the way, which you have to have when you are an emerging team.

◄◄◆►►

TO BE A good hurler you have to have strong character.

You have to be able to assess things yourself, along with what guidance you get. Tommy Guilfoyle was the captain in 1991 but he got injured in an accident at home and was unable to play.

We identified Anthony Daly as a leader very quickly, but Father Willie Walsh suggested John Russell as captain. He had been playing for number of years and would have been older than Anthony. It was felt that we should offer it to him first. We did, but he said no, so we gave it to Anthony then.

He was brash and bold, a great character as he would prove as a player, a manager and now as a pundit. He had that bit of steel about him and you could see it in him early on, and he proved to be a great captain.

Anthony Daly wasn't an outstanding hurler, but he played outstanding games. He got the maximum out of himself and he got the maximum out of the fellas around him. He was very strong in the dressing-room and he got stronger as he went on. We never had discipline problems, but Anthony wouldn't have been afraid to call out players if he needed to. He'd lead anyone and bring anyone with him. There's a great spirit in the Clarecastle club of strong-minded fellas.

◄◄◆►►

ANTHONY DALY

I was more disappointed that Tommy (Guilfoyle) was out because he was such a huge player for us.

I didn't see the captaincy coming. It was something I took in my stride. I didn't play well in the drawn game against Waterford but was okay in the second game, so he left it to me for the start of 1993.

Len used to have these famous meetings after league games.

They could be tough at times. A game might have not gone well the previous Sunday and then everyone would be sitting around at training in Crusheen and he made everyone talk, which was another new departure for us. We were used to only a few guys speaking. Sometimes lads would be whinging because they were a sub, but Len could handle that.

Before a big match he would often call to a lad's house unannounced to get a feeling for where the thing is going, and what we were doing well and not so well. That was huge and before its time. That probably wasn't going on in the bigger counties, that players would have such a close relationship with their manager.

◄ ◄ ◆ ► ►

THERE WASN'T MUCH to show for my first two years. We were beaten by Limerick in the Munster Championship in 1991 but the performance was much more respectable than the year before.

In 1992, we were beaten after a replay by Waterford in the championship. That was a massive blow after all the work we had put in.

We did make marginal improvements, but it wasn't until 1993 when we really got going.

I didn't feel under pressure that year, but I knew myself I'd want to be doing something about the results. It didn't help that I lost two of my selectors, Willie Walsh and Ger Loughnane, who came on board for '92, who were dropped by the county board.

◄ ◄ ◆ ► ►

BISHOP WILLIE WALSH

Ger was managing the under-21s and they lost a Munster final narrowly to Waterford with a team that carried a lot of expectation in the county. The board weren't happy with that and dropped myself and Ger. They decided that selectors would have to be elected by the county board from then on, but Ger and I said we wouldn't stand for election under those circumstances.

◄◄◆▷►

HAVING TO GET new selectors for 1993, I managed to get Tim Crowe and Enda O'Connor.

We beat Limerick in the first round of the Munster Championship in Ennis where Ger 'Sparrow' O'Loughlin had a big game.

Sparrow wasn't that fast, but he had good hands and had an eye for goal. He was on the point of giving up when I arrived. However, Daly and some of the boys got after him to have another go at it and he stayed on, and he enjoyed a great career.

He was a good character and a very nice fellow.

◄◄◆▷►

ANTHONY DALY

Sparrow was only a sub but a clubmate of ours, Alan Neville broke his collarbone with the first ball he went for and Sparrow came on, and scored 1-5.

That was a great boost. The feeling that day in Ennis winning a championship match gave us the belief that there was something stirring in Clare hurling. Even in the parade, myself and John Russell were planning to take out one of the Limerick players after the parade, we were that revved up.

That victory gave us a huge amount of belief, but nobody gave us a chance against Cork in the semi-final. They had come through the trilogy against Wexford in the league final. They were installed as All-Ireland favourites again. We tore into them with no fear and stayed with them, and Fergie Tuohy then kicked the famous goal with his left foot; 'My Left Foot' is what he was known around Ennis after.

◄◄◆▷►

FROM THERE, WE beat Cork in a Munster semi-final to progress to a first Munster final in seven years against Tipperary.

There was a big build-up and a huge wave of momentum behind us that this group of players, many of whom had played in an All-Ireland minor final in 1989, were finally coming of age.

With the Clare footballers having ended their own 75 year wait for a second Munster title when they shocked Kerry in 1992, they thought the hurlers were about to do the same.

However, Tipp were in flying form and they hammered us by 18 points in the Gaelic Grounds. The occasion got to us.

I misjudged it; I didn't realise that the players wouldn't be able to build themselves up for it. I didn't prepare them enough for it. I didn't drive it in hard enough that this was bigger than any other game they had played before.

As well as that, I didn't have them physically fit enough to match Tipp, who had deep fitness levels in them from a few years. They were ruthless that day, they really smashed us.

It was an awful beating.

I remember going into the dressing-room after and I gave them a talking to. We saw that we had to improve a good bit to have any chance.

CIARA GAYNOR

You'd know he was disappointed after a defeat and that he was down, but he'd be very much the get-up-and-go type. Having the farm and so many of us around helped as well. It's not like he'd sit in the chair and be quiet, he'd get up and go out and do something, be it for a walk or take us out for a few pucks or something.

When Tipp beat Clare in the Munster final in 1993, I remember thinking he looked tired.

He'd be disappointed, but he'd have to get up and go to work the next day. That must have been hard for him as he was going off meeting farmers and sure they all loved to talk hurling, but it probably helped as well.

He'd never dwell.

We got a bit of slagging for being involved with Clare in those contests with

Tipperary. Dad is Tipp through and through… he was never anything else. But when he was with a team, no matter who it was, any improvement he made with that team was always for the love of the game of hurling.

Whether that was Clare, Tipp, Kilruane, Shannon Rovers… or the under-6s.

We became Shannon Rovers supporters, and Clonoulty supporters… and Clare supporters. We knew all the lads, having been down there three nights a week with them. You'd support the family and hope Clare would win but you wouldn't be disappointed if Tipp won. We would have been for Clare, but weren't against Tipperary.

Blood is thicker than water and I would have given anything for him to have gotten the team over the line. And when you see the effort he put into it he absolutely gave it everything.

◄◄◆►►

MICHAEL BABS KEATING

I had an understanding of what Len had to do because I was that soldier when I managed Galway in the late-70s. Those of us who are committed to the job, we can understand Len's commitment to Clare.

I bumped into Anthony Daly in Dublin airport the following November and I told him that Clare could win an All-Ireland very quickly. One doubt I had in my mind about that success in 1993 was Clare scored 2-12 that day.

I dwelled on that at successive nights training more than the 3-27 we scored. I didn't run away with myself; from a forwards point of view it was a class performance, I don't think we wasted a ball up front. But to concede 2-12 that day… that would have been good enough to win most matches.

AFTER THAT MUNSTER final defeat, I knew we had to find a little bit more and, strangely enough, I found some of it in an under-21 challenge match between Clare and Tipperary in Nenagh.

I noticed this fellow playing at corner-back and was impressed with him. I found out he was Séanie McMahon, but he couldn't even make the under-21 team as he was concentrating on his studies up to that.

However, I brought him into the senior panel the following year and he turned out to be a great player.

It's amazing how some players can really catch your eye and Séanie caught my eye that night. He was clearing ball after ball. He was a good hurler and had a good head on him. He could read it as well.

Initially, I had him at wing back; he was very young, with John Russell at centre-back but centre-back was his natural position and he developed into a great one after. He could read the game and play the ball. He was sturdy as well and well able to take the tackles.

I'd always look for a good player and hope he would slot into his natural position eventually. You might have a lad corner-back and he would go out to centre-back eventually or vice versa.

We had Anthony Daly full-back and he did well before he moved out to the half-back line and he did even better there.

Brian Lohan came in at full-back and that sealed up that. He was also a very strong leader when he got going, a very stubborn, strong full-back.

Davy Fitzgerald was in goals and he was a really top class goalie. Any night for training I used to leave home early to be in Ennis in good time, and he'd be the first man there and I used to be taking shots at him. And I couldn't put one past.

I was hitting the shots fairly well and right into the corner, but he was able to get to them no matter what. He was a great goalie and fierce dedicated to it; he was stone mad for hurling and still is.

In fairness they came back again in 1994, beating Tipperary in the first round helped by two goals from Tommy Guilfoyle. It was a huge deal to beat Tipperary in the championship, especially after the beating they gave us the year before.

◄◄◆►►

BISHOP WILLIE WALSH

We geared everything that year to beating Tipperary in the Munster semi-final because we were sick from losing the Munster final the previous year, they had destroyed us.

We made such an effort and put so much work into beating Tipperary, and we were fortunate as they were missing some key players through injury in John Leahy and Nicky English, but we never rose for the Munster final and Limerick beat us badly.

We had a great meeting in the month of February and fellas were still sore over the hammering they got in the Munster final the previous year. Séanie McMahon gave an extraordinary speech where he challenged the players and said we'd either go to the grave or beat Tipperary.

ANTHONY DALY

I remember coming off the field and we were delirious.

I often point at that game as one of our biggest wins. Poor John Moroney's death left us with a powerful sense of togetherness. We needed all of that to beat Tipperary because at the time they appeared to be a mile ahead of us after what happened in 1993.

◄◄◆►►

HOWEVER, WE SUFFERED another heavy Munster final defeat to Limerick, which proved to be my last game in charge of The Banner.

I would say I should have done better with them on that day also. Limerick weren't world-beaters at the time, but we didn't match them.

◄◄◆►►

ANTHONY DALY

The Munster final loss to Limerick wasn't anything like the loss to Tipp the year before, which was a collapse.

Everything was done right for us in 1994. The previous year for the final we gathered in the Greenhills Hotel, which houses most of the supporters before the game. After the footballers had won Munster in 1992 there was huge belief that the hurlers would follow.

We had beaten Cork and Limerick, and that was proof alone that we were contenders and there were questions whether Tipp were on the way down after 1992. My brother had flown in that morning from London and I remember meeting him in the lobby with all my family and we walked through the supporters to get to the ground, whereas in '94 in Thurles we were in St Patrick's College beforehand, locked away nice and quiet and had our few pucks.

I felt ready for that final and in the first-half we were every bit as good as them, but we didn't take our chances and Limerick did.

If you move ahead to the following year where we won the Munster title, we got the lucky penalty. Conor Clancy was hardly fouled, and Davy Fitzgerald went up and stuck it away. We needed something like that to happen the year before… a moment to spark something.

◄◄◆►►

I KNEW AFTER that I had taken them as far as I could, and it was time to move on. I went to the county board meeting and told them I was pulling out. They tried to persuade me to stay but it was only manners really.

I knew they really didn't want Ger Loughnane to become the manager, but we had agreed when I appointed him as a selector for the 1994 season that whenever my time was up, that he would succeed me.

Ger had blotted his copybook for many within Clare after they lost the Munster under-21 final against Waterford in 1992 when he was manager of a highly rated squad.

However, I looked for him to come back for the 1994 campaign. The county board initially said no.

I said, 'Well, either he's coming in… or I'm going!'

So, they allowed him to be a selector once more and then when I stepped out that was part of the deal that he would become the manager.

They weren't inclined to give it to him, but they relented and weren't they fortunate they did.

◄◄◆►►

ANTHONY DALY

There was a feeling in the air that Len wanted to give it one more shot.

I was one of the more senior guys at that stage and I would have been quite happy for him to stay on as he handed over quite a lot of the training to Ger in the 1994 season.

I was sorry to see him go to be honest.

GER LOUGHNANE

Two Munster finals and two desperate defeats. Len couldn't have lifted it after that, it needed change both in terms of approach and personnel.

It was a natural finish but all the players that went on to win All-Irelands would recognise the part Len played in their development.

Those four years Len was there, taking out the two Munster final defeats, there was good talent coming through and real quality fellas involved, and those players emerged as great leaders under Len.

The great thing for all those fellas was they came into a good scene from the very start and they learned a lot from Len, about commitment… honesty of effort and decency. If you come into a bad scene, lads could see it as a social outlet but there was none of that with Len. There was very good discipline but not forced discipline.

◄◄◆►►

GER AND I got on well together.

I found him to be a very good coach. He could see exactly what we needed to do, what they needed to do to be successful.

He drove them physically, and he drove their minds as well. He trained them fierce hard so they would be able for anything and they proved to be very successful after.

He was also the personality they needed to really drive them beyond that, and they walked all over Limerick in the 1995 Munster final.

I would have been able to do it too in my heyday, but I didn't like driving them too hard. Ger was ruthless and he did a great job on them. As they say, sometimes it takes a native son to get the final bit out of a team.

I was thrilled for them when they won it all in 1995.

I was at the Munster semi-final against Cork in the Gaelic Grounds when Séanie McMahon broke his collarbone late in the game. They had no subs left and he had to play on at corner-forward. Even with one arm he managed to force a Cork player to concede a line-ball, which led to the winning goal. That sheer bloody-mindfulness said it all about what the players were prepared to do to win for Clare

When the game was over, and they were celebrating under the stand I caught the eye of some of the players and they waved back to me.

I was also in Thurles when they beat Limerick in the Munster final.

◂◂◆▷►

ANTHONY DALY

The traditional thing when Clare won leagues in the 70s and when De Valera was elected Taoiseach in the 20s, were homecomings that took place in the square in Ennis at the Daniel O'Connell monument, and that's where they brought us back to when we won Munster.

We all mentioned the work Len had done in our speeches and eventually this guy appeared in the crowd, and Len was lifted shoulder high by the few people around him.

We couldn't believe he was there and a few of us gave the clenched fist salute to him.

It was bittersweet in that way, in what he had done for me and the development of me as a player and a man, but such is sport. Meeting him after the All-Ireland final, he was invited to a few of the events that were organised.

There was a famous past pupils' night at St Flannan's and all the team were special guests, but he was invited as well. We had great chats with him that night.

Genuinely, he said whatever had to happen I'm happy to have played some part in it and I'm delighted to see ye win it. I knew it was coming and I knew it was belief that was the issue. It can be a fear of victory as well, you don't think there is, but there is, and you have to embrace it when the chance provides itself. And in 1995, we finally embraced it. It changed our lives that breakthrough in '95.

◂◂◆▷►

I KNEW THEY would win a Munster final fairly soon, but I couldn't have seen them winning an All-Ireland as soon as they did.

It was a great achievement for them, and I got a great kick out of it and I was in Ennis on the Monday night when they brought the Liam MacCarthy Cup back after beating Offaly.

They were nice, decent lads and good hurlers.

They didn't have the belief at the time, and I didn't give them enough of that belief. I didn't think I had to drive them as hard as Ger Loughnane drove them, which I should have done but I didn't.

It was essentially the same group of players, but it was a new attitude Ger brought, a more powerful attitude. He drove it into them through hard training. He really gave them hell on the hill.

They were as fit as anyone then, maybe even fitter.

Whether they had the belief or not they were going to be there or thereabouts, and the fitness gave them the belief as well. They were getting to the balls first and were able to do what they wanted to do.

I didn't realise that they needed to be driven more than they could drive themselves. I thought just having them as good hurlers and having their positions right and telling them what to do and all, that would have been enough, but it wasn't. The losing habit was set in then and they couldn't get over that hump, but I could see after that, that's what they needed and Ger Loughnane put it into them.

I didn't feel managing a county team as extra pressure. It was extra work all right and extra commitment but when you're young and energetic you don't feel those things.

When I think about it now, I wonder myself how I did it.

At that time, I just went through it and that was it. I used to go to Ennis through Killaloe, Tuamgraney and Tulla as there was no motorway at that time.

Even though we didn't win any silverware I loved my time there.

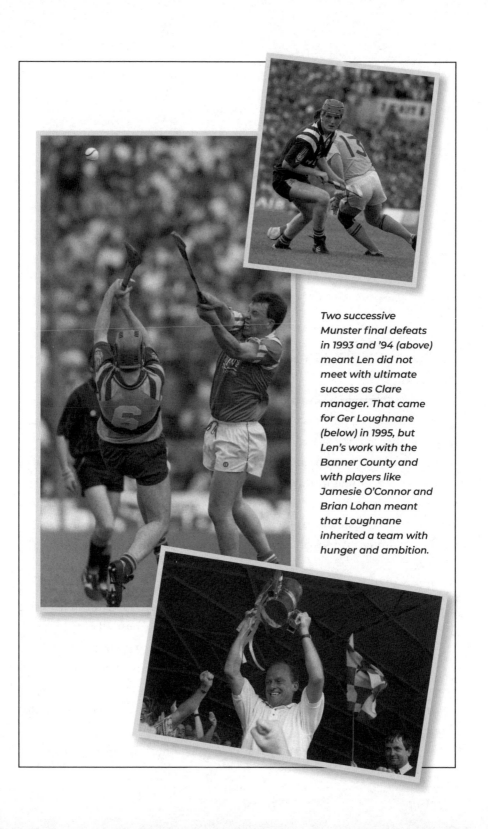

Two successive Munster final defeats in 1993 and '94 (above) meant Len did not meet with ultimate success as Clare manager. That came for Ger Loughnane (below) in 1995, but Len's work with the Banner County and with players like Jamesie O'Connor and Brian Lohan meant that Loughnane inherited a team with hunger and ambition.

« CHAPTER 11 »

Tending to the Grassroots

AFTER FOUR HUGELY enjoyable years with Clare, it never sated my love for the game.

I was still keen to be involved in hurling in some shape, way, or form.

I still loved to see players playing the game and developing. I loved to see them enjoying their hurling as well.

It didn't turn me off having a go at county management again, but it wasn't a desire to get back into it straight away.

It was back to Kilruane after playing and coaching. The next step was into administration where I became chairman of Kilruane MacDonaghs in 1995.

It wouldn't be my idea of hurling, but it was an honour to be asked to take on the role.

It was a lot of work and you have to try and bring everyone together and get everyone working off the one hymn sheet. Once I got used to it, I liked it; raising finance and all that sort of stuff. It is never-ending, you're busy all of the time.

The pavilion at MacDonagh Park in Cloughjordan had just been finished before I went in. That was a big project for us and worked out very well and has been improved on since with a ball-wall and artificial grass with lights; it's great for training youngsters. I was always a club member. I was at every meeting that I could possibly be at all along.

I stepped down as chairman in late 1996 when I became Tipperary manager.

For whatever reason, after the highs of the late 70s and 80s and into 1990 when we won our last North Tipperary senior hurling title until 2018, the club slipped back alarmingly and were relegated to intermediate level in 2000. But came back up in 2003.

I wouldn't say the club took their eye off the ball. Ardcroney National School wasn't functioning as well at the time as regards hurling and we lost a lot of players who never made it, who should have. And that would have reduced our playing numbers quite a bit.

We were very conscious in the club of helping the schools and giving them whatever support they needed. We now have a great principal in Ardcroney, Martin Ryan and he is full of hurling and we were lucky to have the field right beside the school and available for him.

Kilruane National School has always played hurling, Gilbert Williams was great there. He won a number of school titles, and the national school in Cloughjordan was well able to compete. There was also the Church of Ireland school. We asked them and they were delighted to have us in.

Anyway, Ardcroney needed extra help in the early-90s, that's when I began my weekly coaching sessions there, which I continue to this day.

There was no hurling going on in the school at the time. Tom McLoughney was always bringing it up at club meetings to do something about hurling in Ardcroney.

He was right but no one knew what to do, but anyway between Tom and myself, we called a training session one day, and sent word to the school and it started from there, and I have been at it ever since each Wednesday from March through to October.

It keeps you in tune with the youth and with hurling. Management is grand but this is as grassroots as it comes.

Sometimes there'll be a Wednesday where I'd rather be somewhere else, but I won't miss it. I'll be there, even if the knees are at me.

It isn't as easy as it used to be, but the kids are still the same and still love it.

Initially the session used to be for lads 10 years of age and older; now it is for boys and girls from the ages four, five and six. The older players still come but I separate them, and I keep the younger players separate and coach them a bit differently.

Nobody is under pressure to turn up. There'll be no word against you if you miss a night… two nights, or three nights… it is up to the parents and the kids themselves.

But they are still coming and when they run across the field at five to seven each Wednesday, it lifts my heart to see them.

I did get caught one night. I have a couple of grandchildren going to the sessions now and one of them, Colin was six years of age. Anyway, I had a little match going among them and one lad hit a ball up the field and I was behind him.

And I said, 'Good boy Jimmy'.

Colin looked around at me and said, 'You don't know your own grandson!'

I get a great kick out of seeing youngsters hurling and the way to go about it; they would be shouting for frees and they enjoy it.

I like to see, especially the stronger players, when they get good and learn how to solo run, catch the ball, and then hit it.

There is no team, they are just youngsters from the parish. We are not trying to win anything, or we are not trying to beat anyone.

I don't say anything to them, I just say well done and let them hurl away to their own satisfaction. It's a nice way for them.

I remember myself as a young lad that there was no one ever shouting in at me when we were hurling. They all seem to be shouting in now telling them to hit it here and hit it there… do this and do that.

They should be left to themselves a bit more. I let them do that and they seem to enjoy it, tearing up and down the field.

Now I know we are all trying to win when you have a team, but you need to let them think for themselves a bit more and maybe tell them what to do beforehand, but when they go out… Dún do Bhéal.

YOU HAVE TO be conscious of the way you coach youngsters. All you have to do is to go in, encourage them and do a bit of hurling with them. It's vital to get the goodwill of the school to be asked to do that.

However, the fall off at senior level can also be a natural thing where you have peaks and troughs. You have to go with it and try and fight your way back out again.

I would be happy now that the schools are doing very well in the parish. You must get a good group coming together, that's the secret. You'll always come across good lads but it is getting enough of them together to form a team for years, that's the real secret.

Players then would know each other's game inside out. They would be good readers of the game. It's amazing the difference in players.

I remember one little boy in a school, not in our parish. He was very small, but he could read the game inside out. When a player would be going to hit the ball at the other end of the field, he'd be moving over anticipating where the ball would land and sure enough the ball would land there.

Others then wouldn't, they'd start running when the ball is landing. Really good players can read the play and they are a little bit ahead of their opponents all the time. It's lovely to see that but it's rare enough to have them like that at that age.

FROM THAT END, in 1999 when Tipperary County Board were employing full-time Games Promotion Officers (GPO) for the first time, I got a role in the North division.

We would be going around to primary and secondary schools and that was a very interesting time as well, enjoying working with young people once more.

It would have been the first set of GPO's, now Games Development Administrators (GDA) in the county. We had two in the North division, myself and Tadhg O'Connor, with Kevin Halley in the West, Brendan Cummins' father Johnny was in the South and in the Mid there was Dinny Maher, who is now Games Manager, with Andy Ryan now the Mid GDA.

My role suited me down to the ground to visit the clubs and schools to see how they were fixed with coaching and if they needed help.

The secondary schools were an important area. I got involved with Borrisokane Vocational School (now Borrisokane Community College), which is a strong hurling area with players from Borrisokane, Kilruane, Shannon Rovers, Kiladangan, Knockshegowna, Lorrha and some from Shinrone in Offaly.

Tom Moriarty was driving it well and I just gave a bit of help and did a few sessions with them during each term.

I went to St Mary's Secondary School in Newport as well and the Vocational

School in Nenagh and we won the All Ireland 'B' Vocational Schools title in 2008. That was a smashing team that had the Heffernan brothers, Michael and Tommy, as well as Michael Sheedy and Stephen Murray. They beat a cracking team from Coláiste Threasa, Kanturk that contained future Cork players Lorcan McLoughlin and Aidan Walsh, as well as Ciaran Sheehan who played football for Cork and Aussie Rules.

◄◄◆►►

LIAM HEFFERNAN
(NENAGH VOCATIONAL SCHOOL)

We were competing against Nenagh CBS, who had the Harty Cup and that was a huge pull for players.

Len could easily have put his time into another school, but he put a huge amount of years into Nenagh Vocational School.

I remember one day before the All-Ireland final he got them all together, it was about five weeks before the Leaving Cert. The school principal was listening into his talk and Len was getting them going and he said, 'This game is going to be the most important day in your lives... don't mind the leaving cert!'

I don't think the principal was too pleased, but Len said it in good spirit.

◄◄◆►►

I WAS ALSO with the Tipperary Vocational Schools hurling team when they won the All-Ireland against Kilkenny in Ballyragget in 2011.

I also went to the primary schools and when I finished as a GPO I took off and did a few schools on my own time outside of Kilruane, including Ballina and Boher National Schools.

Tipperary hurler, Michael Breen was one I spotted in Ballina. The first day I went in he was there. He was so strong, much stronger than the others.

I had to ask him to hit the ball a bit easier or he'd hurt someone.

His comrade Steven O'Brien, who would win All-Ireland minor hurling and football medals with Tipperary, was there as well. He was equally as good. They were very strong primary school players.

It's hard to pick out players you think might go on and hurl for the county, even at primary school.

They change a lot in a few years, when they get to 14 or 15 years of age they change completely. They can get better or get worse; some of them get heavy and are not able to manoeuvre quickly enough, and some would get very athletic and they are the guys that would make it eventually.

It's hard to spot whether he will make it, or she will make it, it's very hard to do that. You'd see good ones and think... *He'll make it...* and then you'd read the papers a few years later and you don't see his name on the minor team or whatever, they just drift away.

There are big numbers that don't make the grade, but who are still entitled to try it and enjoy it.

Every kid in the likes of Tipperary, which is predominantly a hurling county, should get a chance to play hurling. Now, they can take it or leave after that, it's up to them what they want to do later on. But I think they're entitled to get a chance to play hurling.

They can say that they may end up in a job in Timbuktu or wherever later in life, and if someone asked them where they are from and they say Tipperary, they'll be asked, 'Oh, you must have been a hurler!'

And they can be able to say, 'I was a hurler... when I was young!

That's important, where you come from. It's good to be part of that!

I never reprimanded a youngster if they were hitting the ball wrong or not able to hit it. I'd have great patience with them, and try and get them to get some satisfaction out of it and improve them someway.

That's how I always approach things when coaching kids. I like to see them coming out and playing away, whether they are good or not so good. I like to see them enjoying themselves, hoping they might get a grá for the hurling and stay with it. I am very keen on that, not pushing them to be really good at the time. They have lots of time to develop, but just give them a good liking for it to begin with. Let them have a good experience.

ONE LITTLE GIRL asked me one day, 'Why are you always singing?'

I used to be singing songs in the middle of the matches, and I told her, 'You may as well be happy as sad'.

That would be my way of doing it and trying to have kids enjoying themselves.

Parents might come to you and say, 'My son or daughter is a bit fidgety!' And some of them when they come first would be, and wouldn't know what is going on.

They could be bawling crying one minute and could be pulling on a ball the next minute, so you know you just have to go with them. They get used to it after a while and learn to play. There's great learning in it.

I remember coaching one time in a school and one little lad, no younger than seven, had no interest at all. He had no interest in anything. He might hit the ground a few belts but had no interest in hurling.

One day I asked him to run over to a ditch and back, and I told him, 'I'll time you'.

Another day he came out and he gave a few jumps and banged the hurley off the ground a couple of times, showing me he was a little more alive.

At the end of the match, I was giving out a few credits, such as Player of the Match, and who got the best point… who got the best score… and who got the longest puck. I saw the boy who had no interest in hurling looking at me and I said to him, 'You were the most improved player here today'.

And I meant it because he had improved from what he was.

About two years later, I was giving a coaching course in that young boy's club. This woman came over to me. I didn't know her. She said, 'You told my young lad one day that he was the most improved player on the field'.

She said it was the turning point in his life.

Whatever it was, it wasn't turning towards hurling, but he was just coming alive in himself.

It would frighten you a bit now to say anything wrong to lads and turn them the other way. But it shows you the power of a few words.

You never know.

You have to be careful and a small thing can bring them out of themselves and help them to get going in life and think for themselves.

◂◃◆▹▸

MICHAEL CLEARY
(TIPPERARY SENIOR HURLER 1988-97)

As a young lad in the early 70s I was mad into hurling.

Len Gaynor and Noel O'Dwyer would have come into our shop in Nenagh a bit and if I knew they were coming or thought they were there, I'd be there. Looking at them as a six or a seven year–old I thought they were gods.

I remember my father asking Len one day, 'Would you have any advice for the young fella?'

'Tell him,' Len replied… 'Eat loads of spuds.'

I'd say I ate nothing else but spuds for three weeks solid.

That's why I would always be conscious, when I subsequently became a Tipperary hurler, when dealing with kids. A certain percentage are hanging on to every word you say, so you have to be really careful of what you say in some regards.

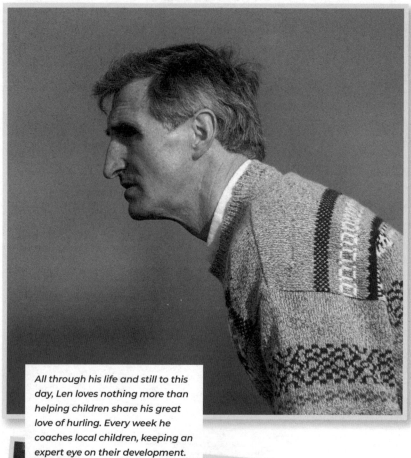

All through his life and still to this day, Len loves nothing more than helping children share his great love of hurling. Every week he coaches local children, keeping an expert eye on their development.

When the triumphant Tipperary senior and under-20 teams visited Kilruane NS in September 2019, Len was invited to celebrate with eight of his grandchildren who attend the school (from left), back – Cormac, Dara, Len, Ava, Thomas; and front, Colin, Keeva, James and Orla.

« CHAPTER 12 »

Answering the Call

AFTER FINISHING WITH Clare and settling back in with the club, I wasn't in a mad panic to get back into management, that was until I was approached to become Tipperary manager.

Séan Fogarty was county chairman in late 1996 and he rang the house one evening but I wasn't there.

Eileen took the call and she told him that I was at a club meeting in Cloughjordan. Well, didn't Séan arrive into MacDonagh Park towards the end of the meeting and offered me the job as manager.

◄ ◄ ◆ ► ►

SÉAN FOGARTY
(TIPPERARY COUNTY BOARD CHAIRMAN 1994-96)

When Babs Keating stepped away after the 1994 championship we were very keen on Len Gaynor but we felt it wouldn't be fair to approach him when he was still committed to Clare, and he had got them to another Munster final at Tipperary's expense.

We felt it wouldn't be the right thing to do to approach him, so we went with Fr Tom Fogarty who was a good appointment at the time, but was probably a little bit premature as he was involved with the minors and maybe a step up to under-21 rather than senior would have been better for him.

Fr Tom was just getting to grips with the seniors when his tenure came to an end. He was very unlucky in 1996 not to win a Munster Championship.

However, once Len was available there wasn't much discussion about looking for anyone else. Even though Len didn't win a Munster or All-Ireland with Clare, they give him a lot of credit for building that team.

That also made it more appealing to us as a county board. Even though Fr Tom was anxious to stay and most of the committee felt the same, they wanted to change some of his selectors but that was never going to happen as Fr Tom said to me, 'I am captain of the ship and if the ship goes down… the captain goes with it'. That was an honourable thing for him to say and showed a sense of loyalty, but I wouldn't have expected anything else.

◄◄◆►►

I DIDN'T HAVE to think twice about the offer. Managing the Tipperary senior hurlers is a close second to wearing the blue and gold jersey as a player.

It's a big undertaking because Tipperary is such a passionate hurling county and to get that job and to be asked to do it was humbling, and I had no hesitation in saying yes.

It wasn't too bad starting off.

The players were all willing and keen. That's the biggest thing. Once you have them interested, it's up to the manager to get the best out of them.

It wasn't as if I ever had to run around looking for lads and drag fellows into training, that didn't happen at all. They were always keen and anxious to play and it was only a matter of time to get them together.

First of all, I had to put a management team in place.

Michael Doyle from Holycross/Ballycahill, son of my former teammate John, had won the All-Ireland under-21 title with Tipperary in 1995 and I thought he was the ideal man for the job as he would be much younger than me and would be better able to relate to the younger players.

◄◄◆►►

MICHAEL DOYLE
(TIPPERARY SELECTOR 1997-98)

The first time I would have come across Len was when he played with my father in the 60s.

I then came across him again in the late-70s when Len was going great with Kilruane MacDonaghs and we (Holycross/Ballycahill) played them a couple of times in county quarter-finals and they gave us good trimmings both years.

Then in the 80s it came full circle after Len playing with the father; he was a selector when I came on to the Tipperary team. They were the barren times, it was like musical chairs in Tipperary at the time – if you weren't successful you were gone, they didn't allow managements to stay too long.

I was with the Tipperary under-21s and we were after winning the All-Ireland in 1995 and were beaten by a last-minute goal by Cork in the '96 Munster final.

Séan Fogarty, who was county chairman, got on to me to ask me would I be interested in going in with Len as we wouldn't have known each other that well.

I was delighted to get involved.

◄◄◆►►

THEN I LOOKED for Murt Duggan, who won an All-Ireland minor title with Tipperary in 1959. Before I ever was planning to be Tipperary manager, I met him one day in Nenagh and unsurprisingly we were chatting about hurling.

I wouldn't have known him at all before that but when I got the job I thought of him as I felt that fella knew his stuff about hurling, and he was from the far end of the county in Ballingarry, but had played his club hurling with Gortnahoe/Glengoole so he knew a fair bit about Mid Tipp as well.

◄◄◆►►

MURT DUGGAN
(TIPPERARY SELECTOR 1997-98)

I was very surprised when he asked me to be a selector.

We were doing a parish journal here in Ballingarry and it was the first meeting we had with the local curate in his house. Len rang my home and my wife gave him the number of the curate's house.

I wasn't thinking about anything like that. I thought it was somebody playing a joke. I didn't believe him at first. I didn't rate myself in that league.

He didn't have to twist my arm and when I thought about it, it was a great honour to be asked. I love hurling and love Tipperary.

◄◄◆▷►

I DID MOST of the training.

I couldn't find anyone to do it. You wouldn't know where to go to look for specific trainers in those days as there was no one coming out of university with the degrees they have now in physical fitness.

Well, none were available that I knew of at that time.

I think I got it fairly right. We did a lot of work in Thurles Crokes Athletic Club, beside Semple Stadium. They gave us the use of their field for winter training as Dr Morris Park wasn't up and running at that stage.

We got on great there, there were a few hills and hollows there which was great for building up stamina. I liked that sort of stuff to put a bit of strain on fellas.

◄◄◆▷►

MICHAEL DOYLE

Len was the manager, coach, trainer, all in one. He was hands on.

He wouldn't have been like the current managers who delegate and have other people in doing all the other stuff.

Murt and I would help out with some of the drills, but Len was hands on most of the time. He was happy doing that. I couldn't picture Len sitting back in the stand and watching training going on; he liked being in the middle of it.

DECLAN RYAN

I was a big fan of Len's because he had brought us to a county title in 1989. I knew the history that was attached to him in his playing days as well as club management.

I knew he'd be a straight-talking man when he came in as Tipperary manager to succeed Fr Tom Fogarty.

He wasn't interested in any rubbish; hurling was the only thing. He was very clear on what he wanted from players in training or in a match.

He was hands on. You didn't come to the field not expecting to work hard. We did a lot of training in Thurles Crokes athletic grounds in the winter and got into Semple Stadium in the summer. He loved running us up and down the mound in the Crokes!

◄◄◆►►

TRAINING AND FITNESS levels had upped a couple of gears in recent years and we had to move with the times. Ger Loughnane and Clare had taken things to a new level in 1995.

Liam Griffin, with Wexford in 1996, worked on the mind a lot. He was very keen on getting their minds strong, like he did when getting them off the bus on the border between Wexford and Wicklow on the day of the '96 Leinster final and telling what it would mean coming back crossing the border again later in the evening as the winner.

The mind works everything, you can be fit as a fiddle but if your mind isn't right you won't perform.

I admire the horse trainer, Aidan O'Brien fiercely. I know nothing about racehorses, but I love watching it on television and I love reading about him.

After one of his horses won a race one day he was asked, did he know the horse would win?

'Well,' he replied.

'I knew he was going to run well because he was training for the last few weeks with a smile on his face.'

I thought that was an extraordinary thing to say about a horse. I know the horse wasn't smiling but he was obviously enjoying his running at training, and it's the very same for a human; if you're in good form and you have the ability, you're going to play well.

There's no doubt about it, but if you're in bad form, you'll be only mediocre or still worse than that. It was a great way of putting it and showed his brilliance at what he does. He gets into the minds of the horses as well.

If you have a team and you know you have them in good shape, mentally, they're going to play well. That's it, and if something distracts them, somebody is sent off or someone is injured and can't play, if that gets into a player's head you have to lift him out of it and get him into the right frame of mind.

In terms of the Tipperary panel, ironically, I inherited a squad that included my own son, Brian, who was there in 1996. Many thought I brought him on but that wasn't the case. He played one great game against Kilkenny marking DJ Carey and he held him to a point.

Initially I would generally look to get a defence organised first of all because if you're leaking easy scores it's very demoralising, no matter what you do at the other end.

People say forwards win matches and they do, but the backs make the forwards in the matches as the backs are supplying the ball to the forwards.

I would have looked at shoring up the defence and getting that tight as possible. We had experience there in Noel Sheehy and Michael Ryan, who were still there from the 1991 team, as well as Conal and Colm Bonner, who ended up at centre-back, even though he was a better midfielder as he liked to run.

We brought in some new faces too, such as Liam Sheedy, who had won an All-Ireland under-21 with Tipp in 1989. He was a good sturdy hurler and that's why I went for him. I knew he would give it everything and those are the type of guys I wanted.

◂◂◆▸▸

LIAM SHEEDY
(TIPPERARY PLAYER 1997-2000)

I came into the Tipp seniors after the 1989 season where I was with the under-21s and juniors that won the All-Ireland titles, but it was only brief for a few league games in late 1989. I was let go before the 1990 championship.

I didn't get back in until the winter of 1996 when Len came on board as manager. It was a long wait, but he probably saw something in me from watching the North championship, and Portroe and Kilruane would have met a lot in the 90s.

We were at a stage where we weren't getting a lot of action so I wasn't getting a prolonged period of training really, so I had a lot of work to do. But Len rang me and said if you are prepared to do the work, I'll give you a chance.

I put in the work and got myself into peak condition.

I was out with the washing in terms of Tipperary hurling only for Len Gaynor so I'll never forget him for placing his trust in me and giving me a chance, because the journey I went on afterwards I wouldn't have gone on with Tipperary only for Len making that call to me in October, 1996.

◄◄◆►►

PAUL SHELLY ALSO came in at corner-back. He was a great character, a bundle of energy. He was very rotund and very strong but was also a very good player; he could read it as well and knew what to do. He ended up a forward, but I had him as a corner-back and he was really good and won an All Star in 1997. He was good craic in the dressing-room as well. His heart and soul was in it and I liked him for that.

Conor Gleeson was also a new face. He was part of the Boherlahan-Dualla team that won the 1996 county championship and, as was the case at the time, they were allowed nominate the captain and they selected Conor.

There was never any interference from any club as regards the captaincy. It was probably hard on him being on the panel for the first year and being the captain, but he was able for it, he was a good, able guy. He was a member of the Gardaí and was well trained, and was a very good hurler.

Brendan Cummins was already on the panel and he stood out as being a really good goalkeeper. He was green at that stage, but he learned very quickly. He was a good shot-stopper right from the start.

Then he got smarter with his puckouts with experience. He was good and we mustered a good defence together in front of him.

Colm Bonnar was at midfield, but we played him centre-back for the All-Ireland final in 1997. Tommy Dunne and Declan Ryan were in the forwards; we had good players, but Clare's fitness probably caught us.

John Leahy was the big name on the panel. He was unfortunate in that he was coming off some personal issues.

However, I had no trouble with him. He was mad for action and played some great hurling but just some small little things that he'd usually do with his eyes closed a few years previous, he wasn't able to do them as well in 1997.

If he had been, he probably would have scored a goal in the Munster final against Clare. He hit the ground instead of hitting the ball. At the time, I thought he tried to do the right thing. Looking back, maybe he had time to rise it, but a split second is all he had to decide.

If he connected properly it was probably a goal but if he didn't the chance was gone, and unfortunately it didn't come off for him.

He was a great hurler, a marvellous hurler with lovely hands and great balance on his feet. He could drift past players and they wouldn't be able to touch him at all. He got some great scores.

A fully firing John Leahy and he certainly would have scored a goal in the All-Ireland final with the last ball he had in his hand. He would have scored that nine times out of 10 but he was right to go for the shot – winners don't settle for the draw.

◂◂◆▸▸

JOHN LEAHY
(TIPPERARY SENIOR HURLER 1988-2003)

It was a big year for me with Len coming in because in 1996 Fr Tom handled all my off the field issues very well, so 1997 was a new start for me.

I can always recall we got into a great conversation in the Hudson Bay Hotel outside Athlone; we went away for a weekend as a panel. We got talking in whatever context and I can remember him asking me how I was getting on?

The one thing he did was he trusted what I was doing to keep myself right physically and mentally. Len said what he wanted to say about encouraging me, telling me to stay at it and that I was an important part of the team.

That's what I needed to hear at the time. To hear that was enough. I didn't need to hear it again and Len knew that.

I remember leaving that conversation and saying to myself… I can focus now on just playing hurling. *Len would have played a part in letting me play my own game. He trusted individuals. He was great at recognising a player's talent and you play to that and develop that, and you are trusted with that jersey*

I would never have looked at it at the time as being a distraction. Len wasn't in my face about it. I worked hard in training and Len said that. He said I was a valuable member of the team. I wasn't in the media, but it could have been stirred up there in that respect.

1996 was a hard year and come 1997 I needed hurling. I could have been dropped and it would have been some void in my life, and I have no doubt I would have found life harder. Even now down the line with sport and people who have difficulty with life, whatever it may be, we need a hobby or something to be interested in and I am forever indebted that Tipperary hurling and Len, at that time, gave me that opportunity to continue having the enjoyment of what I loved doing. That definitely helped me.

If Len had decided not to do that, I have no doubt that John Leahy without Tipperary hurling at that time... my life would have been an awful lot harder. The support that I got all came from Len making the decision that I was to be part of Tipperary hurling and on a personal level it helped me on my journey in terms of not going back down the road of where I was.

That stuff is often taken for granted.

I'm forever indebted to Murt, Michael and Len for that decision.

◄◄◆▷►

MICHAEL CLEARY WAS still there; he was a lovely player but unfortunately for me he was shoving on a bit and he retired after 1997.

I had my work cut out to get him to play but I managed to get him on board as we needed his experience, as the great forward line of the early-90s had begun to break up… Pat Fox, Cormac Bonnar and Nicky English had all retired.

We also had Liam Cahill, who was an All Star forward in 1996 and would become my son-in-law after marrying my daughter, Eimear.

◄◄◆▷►

MICHAEL CLEARY

My father died in January, 1993 and deep down I knew the game was almost up for me then. I played through '93 as that was the year Toomevara nominated me captain.

I don't know how exactly I got an All Star, but I did.

In 1994, Clare beat us in the first round, and we were doing a major renovation job in our shop in Nenagh at the time. The Friday before the match the place nearly collapsed, a major foundation wall fell and blocked off the street and everything.

It was a shock to the system,

I remember the Sunday morning before the game in Limerick telling Babs, I can't play. I was shaking.

Babs said, 'Nicky is out, Leahy is out… will you just hit the frees?'

We were just after annihilating Clare in the Munster final the year before and there was nothing to suggest that Clare had improved in that time, but they went on to beat us.

I remember thinking afterwards how being out of the championship was an ease to me and I had the summer now to get the renovation job done.

In 1995, I was playing moderately well in league games but not anything like where I would have been at my best. Limerick beat us in the first round of the championship, and I remember coming out of Páirc Úi Chaoimh thinking… That's it, the game is up!

I was only 28 at the time but I felt my focus wasn't on hurling, it was on the shop.

I remember going to training some nights and all that was going through my head was the business and whether I had rosters done… did the cheques go into the bank, bills coming and all that. Prior to my father dying, I was a professional hurler in my head, and nothing got in the way of that.

Nenagh Éire Óg won the county championship in 1995 and made me Tipperary captain so I wound up playing in '96 and that was the year Limerick beat us in a Munster final replay and Galway beat us in a League final. I had a very moderate year and said this is it, I'm definitely done.

Then Len took over in the autumn of 1996.

He came into the shop one day and said we are starting (training) in a few weeks and I told him that I was finishing up.

The team was starting to break up and Fox and English had retired, and he asked could you be there on the panel at least. He told me to call out to the house one night and I did, and we sat down for a couple of hours.

My heart was gone out of it to be honest and I said it to him. 'I'm just going to ask you,' he responded, 'Would you come and be on the panel?'

I said, 'Let Christmas come and I'll see how I am.' So I came back in January.

To be brutally honest, only for Len Gaynor I wouldn't have been part of the Tipperary set-up in 1997. My head was gone to a different place and you try and convince yourself it hasn't, but my focus at that stage was the business.

I played some good league games in 1997 against Kilkenny and Clare. That game in Ennis was the most violent hurling match I ever played in. I was at full-forward.

Despite some decent performances I still felt I was only being picked on reputation. I had a decent enough game at full-forward against Limerick in the Munster semi-final, scoring a goal. Then in the Munster final against Clare we got cleaned out.

I lost my place effectively for the All-Ireland quarter-final against Down in Clones but got my place back for the semi-final against Wexford, and had a good last quarter of an hour before I had a shocker in the All-Ireland final.

LIAM CAHILL
(TIPPERARY SENIOR HURLER 1996-2007)

When the management position had come up and the name of Len Gaynor was being bandied about, it was seen as a real injection in the arm type of appointment for Tipperary at the time.

He would have been seen as a no-nonsense manager, who would come in and bring a bit of fire and pride back into Tipperary hurling.

We had struggled a little since 1991 and the team was ageing but to the younger players who were on the panel like myself, he would have been seen as a rigid and regimental type of character, and they were my first impressions of his approach.

This fella is going to set standards and is not going to pussy-foot around anybody. I got the vibe from day one that you are here but don't think that what you have done in the past is going to give you any brownie points to be in my plans. You either work your way into them or you are not going to play.

When he did come man-to-man and speak, which he didn't do that often, you could see the other side of him as a reassuring figure.

I remember going into training one night after getting into a little bit of bother over the weekend in a nightclub in Clonmel. I had five stitches over my eye, and I was afraid for myself going into training.

Selector Murt Duggan was from my own club Ballingarry and he knew what was after happening as it had done the rounds of the parish.

I togged out beside Declan Ryan and he was laughing, asking me what happened, knowing full well I was in trouble. I went out of the dressing-room and out under the tunnel.

And Len was waiting for me.

'Are you in bother?' he asked me.

I said, 'No.'

'What happened you?'

I said I was talking when I should have been listening or something like that.

I was waiting for him to fly off the handle, but he didn't and just gave me a proper civilised chat for a few minutes, reminding me of how I should behave. After that he just said that's behind us and let's get going and there was no more said about it.

Declan Ryan was coming out of the tunnel behind me and was chatting to Len, who said to him, 'That lad (Cahill) is a lunatic… but I like him. I like streetfighters'.

Len had that side to him too of being a character, but he wouldn't show it that often.

◄◄◆►►

OUR FIRST CHAMPIONSHIP game was a Munster semi-final against Limerick, and it was huge as they were Munster champions.

It was a great start for us to get us focused and we had put a lot into it, training 94 times from the first night we got together to that game, because Limerick were sort of a bogey team as they had beaten us the year before in the Munster final, after a replay, and we weren't expecting it.

I always try to get the best out of players and ask them to get the best out of themselves, and I talk to them and bring it out for them.

That's the big thing as regards management. You can't just drive them in and say look, you have to do this and you have to do that. You have to try and talk with them. They were very responsive and very good, but we just lacked that little bit extra.

The win over Limerick set up a Munster final against Clare in Páirc Uí Chaoimh, a game which ignited the rivalry between the sides up to the turn of the millennium.

A National League match earlier in the year had an edge to it and neither side wanted to yield an inch. We won 1-10 to 0-12 in a match played in May and the low nature of the final scoreline was a reflection of just how physical and attritional the game was.

◄◄◆►►

GER LOUGHNANE

The first massive confrontation wasn't the Munster final in 1997, it was the league match in Ennis earlier in the year and it's one I will never forget.

The first thing was the game was put back 20 minutes because of the crowd of 15,000 people that came to see it, even with the game being played on a Saturday night. I went down to the referee's room to speak to Pat Horan from Offaly and I can still remember him in the room beforehand, and he was shaking. There was an atmosphere before the game that you knew something was going to happen.

People talk of the Munster final replay in 1998, but this was way worse because it lasted for the whole game.

It was ferocious stuff.

Tipp beat us that day and that game convinced me we had no business taking on Tipperary physically; we had to out run them and that was the only hope of getting the better of them, and we did that in the Munster final.

To be fair, Tipp's attitude under Len was spot on.

He was so suited to Tipperary and did a terrific job with that team and got the most out of them. However, he made a fatal error in the All-Ireland final by not playing his future son-in-law, Liam Cahill because going back to that game in Ennis, Frank Lohan was on Cahill and was sent off.

I passed Cahill, and he had a big smile on his face, and I said to him, 'We'll get you yet,' and he just laughed at me.

He had the right mentality for taking on that Clare team.

◄◄◆►►

CLARE WERE AT their peak at that stage.

They played great hurling in the Munster final and a goal by David Forde proved to be the difference. However, we were there within shouting distance at the end and John Leahy got a chance to level, but it didn't happen.

Clare's greater fitness told in the end. I was aware that they were fitter than us, so we would have to be better hurlers.

Also, I saw the other side of Ger Loughnane and the lengths he and Clare went to, to win. We had a player by the name of Philip O'Dwyer. He was the up-and-coming player and scored lots of goals for Boherlahan-Dualla to win the county final in 1996 and also scored a goal for Tipperary in the 1995 under-21 All-Ireland final against Kilkenny.

In the 1997 Munster semi-final against Limerick, he played well and had an eye for goal. He was set to start again but we tried to keep him under wraps before the ball was thrown in, as he was highly strung. We were expecting fireworks.

However, the Clare players and management on the sideline got into his head anyway and he wasn't able to function as he should have been able to.

I was aware that Ger Loughnane and the Clare boys would target him, as he was the danger man. They were ruthless in that way.

We had to take Philip off in the end.

1997 was the first year of the back door in the hurling championship and within hours of that Munster final loss, we had refocused. We knew we had a second chance and I spoke to them after the match and said we have to put it behind us, and get going again.

We played Down in the All-Ireland quarter-final in Clones and played fairly well. Down were quite good at the time but Tipp had a good win, 3-24 to 3-8, setting up a semi-final against defending champions, Wexford.

We were like lambs to the slaughter going in against the All-Ireland champions, we were being written off. We knew it was going to be a big challenge and we knew this was going to be hard. But we worked to be ready for it.

We weren't going to be afraid of them. We worked on our own strengths to build ourselves to be able to give a great performance.

We knew before the semi-final that Clare were waiting in the final as they had beaten Kilkenny the week before, and after they beat us in the Munster final, we didn't want it to happen again.

It was easy enough to motivate the players and get them to the pitch of the game. We had them in right shape. We didn't begrudge Wexford winning an All-Ireland in 1996, as long as it was not at Tipp's expense. They deserved an All-Ireland in 1996 and they earned it.

Martin Storey was in his pomp; Larry O'Gorman, Adrian Fenlon and Liam Dunne too. They were a very strong team and we played very well to beat them.

John Leahy got a great goal in the first quarter of an hour. He drifted away from everyone and just flicked a high ball that looked to be going wide past Damien Fitzhenry. Brian O'Meara got the second goal.

It was probably the best performance of my two years in charge of Tipperary. We never looked like losing the game from the start. We were really strong, and strong in the mind as well. We really took them on.

I liked that sort of a challenge, you know, when you're playing someone big like that.

LIAM SHEEDY

The All-Ireland semi-final against Wexford was the biggest game I had played in at that stage. In the first few minutes I was a small bit stuck in the headlights as it was a massive crowd and massive occasion.

I had only just come back into the team as I missed the latter stages of the league through injury. I remember Len coming across the field and telling me to, 'Get your head up and get hurling'.

He focussed me back to all the hard training we had done on the Devil's Bit and all the preparation we had put in, and those few words transformed my thinking. The longer that match went on, I didn't want it to end.

I could have ran forever. If Len hadn't made that run across the field, I could have been getting the curly finger instead.

◄◄◆►►

BACK IN 1997, the National League was played through the summer months and we qualified for a semi-final against Galway in Ennis. However, the game was a week after the All-Ireland semi-final and two weeks before the All-Ireland final, so I wasn't taking any risks and sent out a weakened team and were well beaten.

During the game we were making a substitution and I walked in four yards on to the pitch to meet the player coming off, and I thought nothing of it.

However, three days before the All-Ireland final I found out from Croke Park that I was suspended from the sideline for encroaching on to the pitch against Galway.

It was a real set-up job.

It upset me because it happened so close to the final and I wasn't expecting it. I knew I was being done and I knew it was being done deliberately, as Ger Loughnane was being suspended from the sideline as well for something that happened after their All-Ireland semi-final. So, it was a matter of evening things up by the authorities, to calm things down.

I know for a fact that despite the game being in Ennis, it wasn't the Clare County Board who reported me. I have a fair idea who did it as I saw a certain man at the game and I was surprised to see him there, and thinking about it after… I'm fairly certain that's the person who reported me.

◄◄◆▷►

GER LOUGHNANE

It was a cop out.

They couldn't have me sitting down in the All-Ireland final and Len up and down the sideline because they knew what was going to happen, so they suspended him for some trivial thing, it was ridiculous.

You had no Maor Foirne at that time, so the manager had to do what the Maor Foirne does now. There was no one else going on to the field except the manager.

The strangest thing of all was they had us on specially painted seats, but the paint was still wet when we sat down on them. That added to the craziness of it and it ended up that we both abandoned our seats during the game.

MURT DUGGAN

When we went out before the start of the game there was an old wooden bench with room for four or five people on it. It was a lovely green colour and as it turned out it was freshly painted.

I kept the bottom of the tracksuit and it's still around the house somewhere, and there is a fine slap of green paint on it.

Len got very annoyed at one stage and was going to throw the bench into the Cusack Stand. It was a distraction we didn't need.

◄◄◆▷►

THE SUSPENSION KNOCKED me off my focus and it shouldn't have got to me as much as it did. The powers-that-be decided they would put both of us in seats behind each dugout from where we could communicate with our selectors, and weren't to stir out of them for the game.

However, no sooner had Ger Loughnane left his seat to move on to the sideline than I did the same and nothing was going to stop the both of us.

There was a big cheer from the Tipp crowd when I made my way out of my seat.

After the Munster final defeat, we made a number of personnel changes, including bringing Liam McGrath in at wing-forward in place of Kevin Tucker, who had scored three points from play off Anthony Daly in that game.

Despite that, I felt we needed more power in the half-forward line. Looking back on it, Kevin was a good hurler and we probably should have persevered more with him. He was a very fast hurler and clever. He would have helped out coming back down the field and he would have played well in the All-Ireland final if we had him there, particularly when David Forde came on and played as a fourth half-forward.

Kevin had pace and energy, and was able to get up and down the field very fast, and he would have added a bit more to it.

Clare had four half-forwards in the second-half, but we left Michael Ryan back inside deliberately and asked him not to come out as I was afraid of conceding a goal. Actually, he cleared more ball than anyone in the last quarter of an hour.

If we had won, he probably would have been Man of the Match.

People have asked why he didn't follow Forde out and Loughnane said it to me after too. 'I thought you would have sent out Michael Ryan... we were hoping to get Jamesie O'Connor in there for a goal.'

I was happy enough with the decision to leave him back there and keep the full-back line intact, as if a goal goes in, you're done.

It was unheard of that time to have a fourth half-forward so that was another area where Ger Loughnane was ahead of his time. We weren't for opening the full-back line and Mick cleared the world of ball but unfortunately David Forde did a lot of damage.

We played really well in the first-half and were leading 0-10 to 0-6 at half-time but immediately, at the start of the second-half, Clare upped their game quite a bit. Liam Doyle came up the field and scored a point from wing back which was very inspirational at that point and they got ahead of us.

Then we started to bring in some subs, including Liam Cahill and he scored the first goal. It's one of my regrets that I didn't bring him on a little earlier as he was in great form and could have made the difference as our forwards really struggled in the second-half.

He wasn't going out with my daughter, Eimear at the time; if he was, I would have had no choice but to bring him on earlier or probably have had to start him!

◄◄◆►►

LIAM CAHILL

I had a decent league campaign and started the Munster semi-final against Limerick and did okay. The Munster final against Clare hurt me. I felt the management formed an opinion of me after that game.

Len was a fella where it would take a lot to change his opinion of someone and that game was poor for myself, but also for one or two players that he stayed loyal to.

It would have disappointed me that he stayed loyal to other players that weren't cutting it, especially coming up to the All-Ireland final, but at the time I had no problem with that.

Between the Wexford game and the All-Ireland final I was absolutely flying in training. I knew I wasn't going to start but I thought the way things were progressing in the game, I'd get in fast.

Tipp were getting hammered in so many areas in the forwards after five minutes of the second half and they could have made some changes earlier – bar Eugene O'Neill, who was giving Brian Lohan enough of it but was getting nothing from the referee.

◄◄◆►►

EUGENE O'NEILL GOT the second goal, reacting quickest after a Tommy Dunne '65' came back off the crossbar.

Eugene was a good forward and should have gotten a few more frees that day. He had a good character about him, and you needed someone like that on Brian Lohan. He was a strong-minded chap, and a very good hurler.

I'd never worry about a lad like him going in, no matter who he was going on. You knew he was able to take care of himself, but he got it rough that day and was tumbled upside down and got no frees. It seemed to me at the other end of the field Clare were getting them a little handier, but that's the way it panned out.

We had them caught when Eugene's goal put us a point up inside the last five minutes, but they had levelled before the television pictures came back. Davy Fitzgerald took a quick puckout and we weren't ready for it. Ollie Baker hit it straight over the bar to level it again.

It was the quick puckout that really killed us as we gave away our lead in a couple of seconds. That was the key one, we should have sat on them at that stage.

After Jamesie O'Connor gave Clare the lead, we had a couple of chances near the end and John Leahy got a great chance. It opened up and Fitzgerald made a very good save. He stood his ground well.

There was talk after whether John should have gone for the point to level it and take it to a replay, but he was right to go for the goal because the goal was on and nine times out of 10 John would have scored it.

He didn't hit it that well, but that was that.

JOHN LEAHY

Initially people would have asked, 'Why didn't you put it over the bar?'

I would honestly say I wasn't thinking of whether this chance would win or lose the All-Ireland, I didn't even know how much time was left.

I remember cutting over a line-ball in the county under-21 'B' hurling final in 1988 and I ran off thinking there was about 10 minutes left, but two minutes later the game was blown up.

So, I would say in the All-Ireland final, I wasn't calculating when I got the ball if I would put it over the bar to level it.

I was thinking nothing only putting it in the back of the net.

I have no regrets about going for the goal but the one regret I do have is that I didn't shoot to the right-hand side of the goal, Davy Fitzgerald's left.

There's another thing I would have done differently.

Brian Lohan was coming bull-headed to block me. I was going to shoot to the right-hand post, but his approach changed my mind at that split second and I went across goal. I didn't hit the shot as well as I wanted to… though you have to give Davy

Fitzgerald credit for getting down to it.

The thing I should have done was hit it to the right and forget about Brian Lohan.

◄◄◆►►

IT'S TOUGH COMING off the field after losing an All-Ireland final.

It's very painful.

It's a tough dressing-room to be in.

It's very quiet and hard to talk to people and make sense of it all.

In the blink of an eye you are winning it... and then you don't.

It's equally as tough in a losing dressing-room as a player and as a manager.

However, those are the times you have to stand up and take it on the chin.

I didn't hear much criticism personally, but I am sure there were people saying we should have done this... we should have done that.

Conor Gleeson didn't go well but I was adamant that we wouldn't take him off because he was our captain. I felt it would be nearly conceding defeat to take off the captain.

Nowadays, they take captains off for sport, but that was my thinking at the time... that if you take off your captain, you're saying you're beaten.

◄◄◆►►

GER LOUGHNANE

The hurt that was in Len's face when he came into our dressing-room afterwards.

I never saw anyone as devastated before.

When you think of all he had done with Clare, it did take a little away for a while from winning it... here is a man who contributed an awful lot with Clare and to see the devastation.

He gave his heart and soul to win that All-Ireland for Tipperary and he just came up that fraction short.

DECLAN RYAN

Len was in very hard luck in 1997. We could have won the Munster final and the All-Ireland. Clare were at their peak, a tremendous team.

We were in hard luck to meet them at their best that year. They were certainly keen to make up for 1996 when they felt they should have beaten Limerick and they were certainly at full throttle for most of '97.

While we could have beaten them in the Munster final, we played better in the All-Ireland final. Small things either way could have made the difference and you could have been talking about Len Gaynor as an All-Ireland winning manager... as well as a great GAA man.

MICHAEL CLEARY

I can't imagine anyone would have ever thought of Len Gaynor as a man with an agenda. What he says and what you hear, is what he means.

That came through in his hurling and in my year with him with Tipperary, it was about working hard, playing hard, carrying the tradition of the jersey with you. It was a no frills, no nonsense approach and I like that.

Much like Napoleon, he was unlucky with Tipperary.

He was unlucky in 1984 and '85, they lost two great Munster finals to Cork. 1984 was a freak and in '85, they played really well but Cork were just a good team. Subsequently you could see Tipp were coming but they were just unlucky.

There's great credit due to him in 1997 because he went within a hair of winning Munster and All-Ireland titles with a moderate enough Tipp team.

◄ ◄ ◆ ► ►

COMING INTO THE 1998 campaign, the pressure was on.

Defeat in an All-Ireland final takes a lot out of you. It's hard to motivate a team early in the year but had they got over that match they probably would have gone on.

I didn't have any trouble in getting the group into training, but to get the right tone was harder. The enthusiasm would be a bit lower. Losing an All-Ireland final by a point; it drains the energy and confidence out of you.

We also lost Noel Sheehy and Michael Cleary to retirement, two great players for Tipperary but also great leaders and those kind of players are hard to replace in a dressing-room.

However, we lost to Waterford in our first game which was a Munster semi-final and that was it… our season was over in June.

We would have been expected to win that game. We did everything bar score and we were very unlucky to lose by three points.

There were new players on the team, including Aidan Butler at centre-back and he looked the part. He was a big strong man. It allowed us to release Colm Bonnar back to midfield.

We weren't at the races really.

We had done our best and that's the way you have to take it.

I didn't know after the match that I wouldn't manage them again, but I sensed it alright.

◄◄◆►►

DECLAN RYAN

Having done so well in 1997, we were caught a little bit on the hop against Waterford in '98. Again, going back to having that bit of luck, we hit the post, we hit the crossbar… we did everything bar score that day.

Liam Cahill hit the crossbar with a shot that rose 100 feet into the air he hit it so hard. We also hit the side-netting at the end of the game. Had we got over that game we could have learned from '97 and got back into the All-Ireland series again.

LIAM SHEEDY

There was a group of players at the time that didn't step up. If they had their time back again, some of those boys would have carried themselves differently.

Ultimately, the leadership must come from inside the white lines and some of the sideshows that were going on were outside of Len's control.

I don't know if the playing group fully stood up behind Len Gaynor like they should have done in 1998 and unfortunately it was a cut-throat business that time, where if you lost your first match you were out.

It was a disappointing way for Len to finish.

He was a very credible manager, and was a hugely honest Tipperary man. He had no hidden agenda, he just wanted the team to do well.

◄◄◆►►

I WOULD HAVE liked to have stayed on, but I didn't get a chance.

Nicky English rang me at the house one day in early August. I was about to get in the car to go and watch Ciara play in an All-Ireland semi-final against Galway at Nowlan Park.

Nicky said that he had been approached to take the job to be the next Tipperary manager and that he would be taking it.

That was the first that I had heard that my position was under threat. Nobody from the county board had approached me following the Waterford game. I went to the camogie match, and afterwards bumped into the board chairman. I was told that the board had nothing finalised yet and, to the letter of the law, they hadn't as the board hadn't met to ratify what the selection committee was recommending – which was that Nicky would take over.

I understood then, and understand now still, that the county board had a job to do, but I still expected a simple phone call to tell me that I would not be continuing as manager. That would have sufficed.

◄◄◆►►

MURT DUGGAN

I was very disappointed for Len's sake. I was very annoyed about it at the time that it wasn't done properly. It was very blunt. He certainly didn't deserve that.

The team were still good enough and if they had gotten over Waterford, things might have been different.

JOHN LEAHY

I would say Len got a raw deal.

We didn't go from a team that lost an All-Ireland by a point to a very poor team the following year. Waterford were coming alright but would Waterford have beaten Tipp if we had gotten a second chance, I'm not so sure.

Tipperary hurling is cruel.

Len was on a hiding to nothing once Nicky showed an interest.

Nicky is a Tipperary favourite and will always be. Nicky could be seen to do no wrong in that respect and Len would have suffered because of that.

If Nicky put his hat into the ring for the Tipperary job today, he'd still get it.

I NEVER THOUGHT anything less of Nicky English after the whole episode. He proved himself to be a good manager, but it took him three years before finally winning an All-Ireland in 2001.

Nicky learned his lessons from 1999 and 2000, and built them into a right good team after.

I wouldn't have any animosity against anyone because it is only a waste of time.

I was bursting to win an All-Ireland with Tipp, but it didn't happen.

Once it's over, it is over… there's no going back then, you have to take it and move on somewhere else in life.

So, it was the end of my managerial career with county teams at senior level.

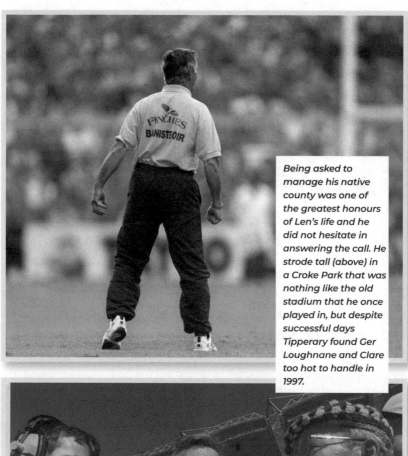

Being asked to manage his native county was one of the greatest honours of Len's life and he did not hesitate in answering the call. He strode tall (above) in a Croke Park that was nothing like the old stadium that he once played in, but despite successful days Tipperary found Ger Loughnane and Clare too hot to handle in 1997.

« CHAPTER 13 »

More Strings to the Bow

EVERYTHING WAS AFTER finishing up with Tipperary and I was back with Kilruane MacDonaghs and coaching young lads there and in the schools.

I still had a hand in the pot and that's what I always wanted, to feel a part of it.

In 2005 I was drafted back into the inter-county fold as manager of the Tipperary intermediate team in what was a unique arrangement, where I was also a selector to the under-21 team under manager Fr Tom Fogarty, who was a selector with the intermediate team also.

◀◁◆▷▶

FR TOM FOGARTY
(TIPPERARY UNDER-21 HURLING MANAGER 2005-07)

Len was appointed intermediate manager and a couple of weeks later county chairman, Donal Shanahan asked me would I take on the under-21 team.

Len had already asked me to be a selector with the intermediates and I said I wasn't going to refuse him. But when I was offered the under-21 job, I asked Len would he be a selector with the under-21s as well and he said of course. And I was delighted to have him.

He added the stamp of approval and respect straightaway.

Even though he was a long time retired, the players would have heard of him because the man continued to coach teams long after he finished playing.

He was a great man to give a speech in the dressing-room. He was really good at motivating players and that's important. You can have all the All-Irelands you like, but if you don't have the communication skills to get the best out of players you won't make it as a coach.

Len had that and was able to get guys to perform to their maximum which isn't easy to do.

◄◄◆►►

THINGS HADN'T CHANGED that much from 1998 but players were becoming more aware of what they could do.

Television was huge, where they could see all the different sports and see how fellows improve and how to win matches, be it in tennis, golf, rugby or whatever.

The modern ways of training teams were starting to come in, including getting players fitter. It's more important than ever nowadays but it certainly had moved up a few gears at that stage. All these lads and girls were coming out of college with their degrees in fitness and all that sort of stuff.

They started coming on board county teams and the whole thing has changed from then. Players are much fitter now and are getting even fitter as the years go on. It's a combination of everything including lifestyle as much as training, eating the right foods... doing so much right.

In terms of players being distracted by modern issues such as work or socialising, I didn't notice it but I presume it was there. Fr Tom was better able to spot those things and deal with those outside distractions.

He was good at that. He was very good at communicating with players. You need good, strong characters when the game is in the melting pot, no matter what level you're at. To win this thing... are you going to surrender... or are you going to fight?

Anyone can hurl when things are going right.

Tony Wall always used to say that. It does run right for you some days but when it is not running right, you must fight and battle your way out of it. Those were the characteristics Fr Tom would look for and I would look for as well.

In 2005 we won two games in the Munster Intermediate Championship but were defeated by Cork in the final and the Rebels did likewise in the under-21 final in Páirc Úi Chaoimh, where the concession of four goals undermined us in a 4-8 to 0-13 defeat.

We remained in situ for the 2006 campaign but once again Cork proved too good in the Munster intermediate final. But we finally got one over on them in the under-21 final, winning 3-11 to 1-13 – Tipp's first Munster under-21 success since 1999 and a badly needed one at the time.

We nearly won the All-Ireland final at Croke Park; we drew with Kilkenny, conceding an equalising goal with the last puck of the game.

We were in a strong position, but we did sit back late on and we didn't cop it in time. You have to hurl on rather than hold on, because a sliotar can move so fast and it can take a deflection or anything. You can get a goal out of nothing.

In soccer or rugby you can hold on, but in hurling it is so easy to get it from one end of the field to the other in a flash, that you have to play on and keep your system in place and play it out to the finish.

We didn't and they got one final shot. Richie Hogan scored the goal.

It was a tough day as not only had we given up a winning position in the under-21 final, Ciara lost the All-Ireland senior camogie final as that was the first time the under-21 hurling and senior camogie finals were played together at Croke Park.

Kilkenny won the replay in Thurles a week later. It was a hard way to lose. Kilkenny had a star-studded team with Richie Hogan, Cha Fitzpatrick, Richie Power and TJ Reid.

We hurled really well to nearly beat them. Conor O'Brien was on that team, with Paddy Stapleton, James Woodlock, Darragh Egan, and all those fellas were good committed hurlers.

It was great to see so many of those guys push on and win senior All-Irelands with Tipperary. It's lovely to look at players you had something to do with early on in their careers and then to see them blossom as senior players.

Conor O'Brien was the best man I ever saw to retrieve a situation.

If his man got the ball or another man was going through, time after time he got back and saved it with a hook, block, or a flick. He was terrific at that.

I STEPPED AWAY as intermediate manager for 2007, but Fr Tom stayed at the helm at under-21 but we were beaten by a last second point by Cork in the Munster semi-final and so that brought down my involvement with Tipperary – starting out as a player with the minors in 1962 and finishing as a selector 45 years later.

Between all the teams in a coaching capacity it totalled 17 years, beginning with the minors in 1971.

I ENJOYED IT all.

I didn't enjoy losing though. It was always painful, but you get over it. You learn to take it and that is part of the character as well. You have to be able to take that because everybody loses far more than they win, as managers or players.

In all my time I never really had a big disciplinary decision to make which was a relief and I'd like to think that was down to the respect all the players afforded me.

If I had to drop someone from a panel or leave them on the subs bench for a game, I talked to them before I announced the team to explain what we were doing.

There's no point in going in and announcing a team and saying that's it. If you want to make changes you have to let the players know, and keep them in tune to what's happening and why it is happening. I liked to head off things before trouble could fester, as if you don't and let things run and run, then you're going to have a problem.

You must be in tune with the players.

You have to be aware what the difficulties might be or what the difficulties could be on the day of the match, and know how we are going to get there; have all that clear and easy for them so they don't have to worry about it.

I ALSO ENJOYED a stint in the media, working as an analyst and co-commentator with RTÉ Radio.

I don't know how that came about but I got to like it. I got on well with Mícheál Ó Muircheartaigh. I wouldn't have known him well before that. Brian Carthy is a very nice man as well and I got on well with him too.

I got to go to matches all over the country and you had the best seat in the house watching them. You had a great chance of reading the game and could see the overall picture, whereas on television you see exactly what's happening where the ball is but you don't see what is going on either side of it... who's moving or who's not moving.

I didn't do much preparation; it was just straight into it.

I wouldn't open my mouth unless I was asked to, but I would point out things such as there's only two forwards in there or if one man is gone back into the backs as a sweeper. That sort of stuff was coming in around that time.

I couldn't understand that really and I still don't. Five forwards trying to beat seven backs... it doesn't make sense.

I liked radio; I wouldn't have been keen on television.

It isn't what you say on television, it is how you look when you are saying it. Viewers can see every part of you. It's alright once you get used to it and you relax and just talk as if you're talking to the one person. I only did it for a few years, but it was nice experience.

I like radio all the time, I liked it going back the years when Michael O'Hehir was broadcasting the matches, he brought great life to it. You could feel you were at the game when you listened to him. Mícheál Ó Muircheartaigh was much the same, he brought his own unique way of speaking and bringing the game to people as well.

You have to paint a picture and try and tell the full story of how the game is developing. I was conscious of painting a picture for people who can't see the game because it's the overall story that matters, of how a score came about and who made it, whether it was a mistake or not.

A score doesn't just happen, there's always a story around it.

I liked to bring that into it if I could and I would also be fair, as well, to everyone. The players are doing their living best out there. I would never say this player is hopeless, rather I'd say his opponent is getting on top.

◄◄◆►►

BRIAN CARTHY
(RTÉ RADIO)

Len was a superb analyst. His knowledge of hurling was second to none. He was always so incisive. I also enjoyed his humour and witty comments and the listeners did too.

Anyone listening to RTÉ Radio would know instantly that Len had an innate knowledge of the game but also had the ability to relay what was unfolding on the field of play.

That is not easy; he called the game as he saw it, without fear or favour, while at the same time he was always very respectful to the players and the managers.

That came about due to the fact he played at the highest level for so long but even players who would have played at that level, it is not easy then to transition to being a co-commentator and seeing what is unfolding on the field of play.

Hurling, no more than Gaelic football, has changed over the years and he understood it innately and understood the twists and turns of the game, and was able to articulate that on radio. If a team was leading eight or nine points and suddenly 15 minutes later the game has changed… Len could isolate it immediately about why it happened.

He was never looking back and was always looking forward to the future, to the players of the day showcasing their skills.

He always had that great understanding of defensive play, also, because sometimes we probably praise the forward for the great scores and sometimes we underestimate great defensive play, the blocking, hooking and tackling, that's where Len came into his own.

When he finished his county managerial
career Len found time to afford people
throughout the country, and not just
in dressing-rooms, the full extent of his
knowledge of the game and joined RTÉ
as a co-commentator with Mícheál Ó
Muircheartaigh and Brian Carthy (left).

« CHAPTER 14 »

From the Sideline to the Stand

THE END OF my time as Tipperary manager in late 1998 came just around the time I entered a new phase in my hurling story…. the proud dad.

I have always been proud of each of my children, no matter what they have achieved in both life and sport, but seeing one of your own win an All-Ireland medal at Croke Park, like I did, was a different feeling altogether.

All my kids were interested in hurling and camogie and played with Kilruane MacDonaghs.

Brian was a lovely hurler. Much better than I was. He had good hands and plenty of courage. He played senior hurling with Kilruane MacDonaghs for 18 years and, like me, ended his career playing junior hurling for the club.

He played on the Tipperary minor team that won the Munster final in 1991. Tipperary went on to be beaten in the All-Ireland minor final that year. After playing under-21 for Tipperary, he graduated on to the senior panel in 1994 and would eventually find me as his manager in 1997.

In early 1997, he suffered a broken finger in a match and a screw had to be put into it. When it was time to remove it, the medical personnel could not get the screw out. In the process, the finger broke again. The finger eventually healed in a crooked position making it very hard to catch the sliotar.

He went on to win a Munster final with the Tipperary intermediate team and they were unlucky to lose the All-Ireland final in 2002, following a replay against

Galway. He also got two caps for Ireland, playing shinty against Scotland. Brian had a great career with some sterling performances for Kilruane MacDonaghs.

Nowadays, with his own children coming along, he is very involved with the club and coaches the under-8s and under-10s.

HOWEVER, THERE WAS something about Ciara from an early age that I could relate to.

Some people remarked that they see a lot of me in her.

She was very strong and a very good hurler. She'd be boring balls at me, and I'd be able to catch them for a while, until she got too good.

She also had great passion for the game from a young age and like them all, they came with me to as many training sessions with various teams as they could. She got involved in a session one year when she was just six and she did a great job for me.

We were preparing for a North championship match against Lorrha in 1985 but the year before there had been a lot of ill-feeling after a game between the two teams.

This thing was still in the air a year later and I wanted to make sure they were calm and focused on winning and not seeking retribution.

I had them all sitting in the dressing-room and I put Ciara sitting on a chair and I told her to sit there and keep quiet.

I was in the middle of my few words.

And I rhetorically asked, 'Well boys what are we going to do against Lorrha on Sunday?'

There was dead silence.

The next thing Ciara jumped off the chair.

'KILL THEM!' she shouted.

Everyone burst out laughing. She did the job for me and took the whole steam out of the situation I wanted to avoid.

We beat Lorrha the following weekend.

She played in Kilruane national school with the boys and then she played both under-12 and under-14 with Kilruane MacDonaghs as well.

They were playing Moneygall one day and you know the way boys would not like to be marking a girl? She was playing anyway, and she was doing well.

And her man wasn't staying near her… he didn't want to because she was a girl. However, the mentor on the sideline was telling him to get in and mark 'your man'.

Even if it was a girl he was marking.

◄◄◆►►

CIARA GAYNOR

We hurled at home in the yard with him from when we were small.

The craic we had playing hurling at home on the concrete yard in front of the house. There would always be a match after dinner.

He was always doing trick shots and charging us a fiver for every slate we broke. He always made it fun. He always wore a peak cap and would try and distract us if we were coming in with a ball.

He'd throw the cap at us.

He did the same at training with Clare one night when they were short a back-man for a game and he stepped in. One of the forwards was coming in and he threw the cap at him and the player fluffed the ball. Dad cleared it.

That clip of him on Twitter in the ball-alley during the pandemic and his under the leg shot… he always did that as well. He'd also sneak around the side of the house and ram the ball at us. It was always fun.

We'd have to march around the yard like we were playing in an All-Ireland final and he'd be humming the tune the Artane Band would be playing.

No matter what level you played, whether it was for Tipperary or the club, he was always very conscious of us being as good as we could be, bettering ourselves. And no matter what level we played at… whether it was under-12 camogie, junior 'B' hurling or senior county, he'd nearly be the first to tell you what you did wrong after a match.

I might not have seen it as constructive criticism back then, but he'd tell you. You could have scored a few points, but he would tell you about the one you missed and that was him trying to make us as good as possible.

The biggest thing with him was that we enjoyed what we were doing.

◄◄◆►►

FOR SECONDARY SCHOOL, she went into St Mary's in Nenagh and they had a good team. Ger Dullea trained them and they won junior All-Irelands in 1990 and '91 – the latter with Ciara on the team as just a first year.

Three years later they made their breakthrough at senior level on a team captained by Noelle Kennedy. Ciara got great experience there and progressed on to the Tipperary minors and that lifted her game again, winning a Munster medal in 1996. That year she was also chosen by the *Cork Examiner* (now the *Irish Examiner*) as the rising star in camogie to look out for. Their choice worked out pretty well.

Tipperary camogie was in the doldrums at the time.

There was always camogie throughout the county, but it wasn't strong, and it wasn't particularly strong in the club anyway. But it started to gather momentum around that time with the intermediate team winning the All-Ireland title in 1997, with Ciara part of the team that defeated Clare in the final.

It was a win that kick-started the golden era of Tipperary camogie where between 1999 and 2004 they won five All-Ireland senior titles in six years, with Ciara involved in all five successes.

After I finished managing Tipperary in 1998, I started to go to more of their games and I was amazed at how good they were. They were really good players and they hurled like the boys. It helped that in 1999 camogie moved from 12 to 15-a-side for the first time and they played on a full-size pitch rather than just between the two 21-yard lines which had been the case.

They got no chance really up to that.

They were meant to be ladies and lady-like and all this.

There was nothing wrong with their hurling as it always made them look elegant in my eyes anyway. Camogie started to grow then, and it was only right that they get their chance to play the game properly if they wanted, and they took it with both hands.

◄◄◆►►

CIARA GAYNOR

He'd go anywhere to watch a match and the fact that in 1999 when camogie went to 15-a-side and we were using the full pitch, you could compare it more to hurling.

Fifteen aside certainly helped camogie, the skill level went up.

He really enjoyed those matches and then of course the fact we did well for the most part would have helped as well.

◂◃◆▹▸

THEY LIFTED THE whole standard in Tipperary, and camogie in general all over the country, which was great. The girls weren't expected to play rough games or tough games, or whatever we like to call them before that, but they were starting at that time.

They blended into a tremendous team. Una O'Dwyer at full-back, Sinéad Nealon wing back, Ciara at centre-back and Therese Brophy on the other wing. They were a stylish team and a focused team… Suzanne Kelly was there as well at corner-back and Claire Madden and, of course, Deirdre Hughes, Claire Grogan, and Eimear McDonnell in the forwards.

They had to come back from an awful 25-point defeat in the league final to Cork. It was a defeat that would have killed many a team but to their credit they got themselves together after that game and crucially managed to upgrade the coaching team to include Michael Cleary.

They responded to him as well and they lifted their game. He was the ideal man for them because he had a nice manner and he spoke to them well. He drew the best out of them; he didn't try to bulldoze it out of them.

He just drew it out of them and improved their ability all the time and they developed into a great team.

◂◃◆▹▸

MICHAEL CLEARY

Within a week or 10 days after the league final, Sinéad Nealon and Deirdre Hughes contacted me to see would I be interested in getting involved.

Colm Bonnar rang me then and he had been approached as well, and he told me Séan Hennessy was getting involved too and that we all would do one night a week to give them a hand. That was kind of how it happened.

We beat Clare in the first round, then Down in the semi-final. Luckily enough,

Kilkenny beat Cork in the other semi-final which was huge as psychologically the girls knew they could beat Kilkenny – but if it was Cork, they could have been under pressure.

We ended up winning the All-Ireland and in 2000 I was happy to take over as manager. It wasn't that I canvassed for it, it was more like it was left up to me.

I would have spoken to Len a fair bit about certain players. It wasn't as if there was any magic dust in what he said but it was a fierce reassurance to me. It was obviously coming back from Ciara that what I was doing, the players liked.

I remember him saying to me several times, you have a good team, you have a good way about you... and they like you. 'Stay strong and stay determined,' were his words.

I didn't have a clue about management, apart from training some underage teams in Nenagh Éire Óg. I was sure of myself, however, and how the game should be played.

One of the great pieces of advice he gave me was... 'Don't focus on picking the team.. get the players hurling well... and the team will pick itself'.

Some managers can get preoccupied with picking the team and placing the team, but Len said to focus on getting the players hurling well and the team will pick itself.

Ciara was the rock of the team, there was never any question about her place. I got on well with her.

Len and I never had a discussion about Ciara, it was all about the team.

One day in particular stood out, the 2001 All-Ireland semi-final replay against Cork in Limerick. We had drawn in Mullingar a week earlier.

Even though we won three All-Ireland finals, that day was the stand-out for me.

The girls had this thing about Cork. We had beaten them in the 2000 All-Ireland final. The word was coming back that Cork were gunning for us as we caught them with two early goals. It wasn't that we hung on, but the two goals were crucial, and we won by five points.

2001 was the year to decide who was the best team.

Tipperary or Cork?

We got out of jail in Mullingar and I remember meeting Len on the side of the road, and he had the fist up to me.

'Keep them hurling!' he says.

'You've got to make them believe, you've got to beat Cork!' he says. 'Focus on playing well ... and ye will beat them.'

We nearly cried with joy after winning that game.

It was a hugely entertaining four years. They were a group that came together and gelled. All they wanted was a bit of organisation and leadership. It wasn't I that made them better players.

The sum of the parts just worked, and the jigsaw came together, and I happened to be in the right place at the right time. I happened to be a good fit for the girls, and it worked well.

CIARA GAYNOR

We were very good with the bunch of lads we had in with us for the 1999 final. Michael Cleary and Colm Bonnar had us so well prepared and were so seasoned on the big days that they had us primed.

Dad would have been great that way in that he never tried to push his views on you but there would have been things I would have asked him, and he'd only be too happy to advise.

I'd always come back to him after a match and ask him, 'What do you think?'

He was always very good that way to give a small tip.

If your own child is playing you can tend to focus on them more so. He'd see the small things I was doing right or wrong, so I'd often go to him for advice but he'd never force it on me.

◀◀◆▶▶

THEY MANAGED TO get to their first All-Ireland senior final on a glorious day at Croke Park in what was the first year the camogie final was shown live on television.

I got a kick out of being there. It was great to see one of your own performing on the big stage as I did with Tipperary 30 years previously.

I was keyed up for it before the game as if I was going to be playing myself. However, when the game started, I was calm enough. I wouldn't be shouting and roaring, but I would be feeling the tension alright.

I didn't say too much to Ciara beforehand. I used to let her do her own thing and I never pushed any of my children because it's a dangerous thing when the father has hurled before them, and tries to impose himself on them.

I wouldn't do that; I never did that.

But if they did ask me anything, I would give them some advice.

With Ciara, it would just be about pucking in the yard and I might say an odd thing here and there, but other than that I let them at it. If they didn't want to play hurling that was fine, I wouldn't have pushed them into it either.

◄◄◆►►

CIARA GAYNOR

He got a great kick out of the camogie and when we won the first All-Ireland in 1999, he got a greater kick out of that than when he won his own medals and I couldn't understand that at the time. But having my son, Charlie now I'd give every one of my medals back to see him fulfil whatever dream he wants, and I can see that now.

It was easy for dad on the sideline to see what you are doing wrong or who is playing well, as he had a good view from there, but it must have been hard, especially with your own kids playing. Everyone wants their own kids to do well or perform well.

When we started becoming successful, I always felt that the fact I was Len Gaynor's daughter would be mentioned. In a way if it helped with the status of camogie at the time I didn't mind, but I sometimes felt there were players on the team a hell of a lot better than me and they didn't seem to get the same focus.

It wouldn't have bothered me if anyone knew my name or not.

Any time I played, if I was happy with how I played that was enough for me. Obviously, the team came first.

◄◄◆►►

I THOUGHT CIARA was better than me.

She was a lovely centre-back. Maybe I'm biased but I thought she was very good. She held her position well and she covered the two wing backs very well, and she cleared the ball very cleanly.

She had a good strong stroke. She was strong, she might not look that big, but she was very strong, and she was able to hold her own with any opponent.

I saw her in one game and a girl went down the wing and Ciara wouldn't have been marking her, but she took off after her. She would not have been recognised as a speedster, but she caught up to her and the girl tried to turn back to get a shot away.

But Ciara blocked her down and cleared it.

I thought it was a great bit of skill and if you could have taken a video recording of it, it would have shown players that this is the way to catch someone that is breaking through; don't give up, get after them and you will catch them if you corner them.

She had that ability and she had a good ability of reading the game as well.

They were great times following that team all over Ireland for that period in which they won five All-Ireland titles but also lost three finals.

It was a lovely period for us as a family to go to games together because I was finished in management and here was another reason to stay with hurling, which suited me down to the ground.

It was just another phase but a lovely phase.

As I wasn't directly involved, I could relax a certain amount and watch the games and enjoy them. I really enjoyed it and enjoyed all that team, though I was fierce proud of Ciara and how well she did.

It was a very different experience because I didn't expect it and I didn't dream that it would happen. Here it came into our life and we got great mileage from it.

You never know what is going to happen with your family and Ciara turned out to give us great enjoyment.

I knew from being a hurler myself what she was going through, and I knew what she had to do. I never used to fear for her. I had faith in her.

I knew she'd do well.

There's no point in being worried about things. You get on and do your stuff and she had that mentality as well. She was cool and calm about it. She wouldn't be getting in knots over things.

I tried to keep her occupied a day or two before a match, that's what I always believed in; being busy without overloading yourself. You then go out with a clear mind, not worried about something else, just thinking about what you have to do.

Family has always come first for Len and Eileen photographed (above) with their children (back from left, Lennie, Fionnuala, Eamonn, Eimear and Brian; and front, Sinéad and Ciara.

The entire Gaynor family with Fr Pat Greed celebrate Len and Eileen's 50th wedding anniversary in October 2018.

« CHAPTER 15 »

The Evolution of Hurling

HURLING HAS EVOLVED completely since my time playing it, when it was fairly dour stuff at times.

There was some great hurling played as well, great clashes of big men. Big stars meeting each other like Christy Ring, and Mick Mackey before him. Jimmy Smith of Clare, the great Waterford team of 1959 that had Martin Óg Morrissey, Philly Grimes, Seamus Power… they were amazing hurlers.

The game was slower then, there is no doubt about that. We weren't as fit as the modern players, but the ball was heavier. It was unusual that time to score a '65' whereas nowadays they are scoring them for sport.

Everything changes and everything evolves.

The hurlers nowadays are really terrific. I think they are much better than we were because they have better skill altogether and better fitness levels. The ball is lighter and is travelling much better and further.

They have refined the hurleys also. They have shortened them. We always had a 37-inch hurley and once you were over 18 years-old that was your length, even for a small man. Up to recently you measured the length of your hurley to the length of your leg, up to your hip, but that has changed.

It is also a game of rising the ball now.

There are very few ground strokes now… like Seamus Callanan's goal against Wexford in the 2019 All-Ireland semi-final. You don't need that longer hurley anymore. In my time the heavy hurley would hit the heavy ball and drive it.

I admire today's players greatly.

Their skill is unbelievable… the catching of the ball, the striking of the ball, blocking, hooking… all that has improved immensely from our day.

The scores they are putting up now are phenomenal. It's all 20-plus points and whatever goals you can get as well. It's now getting up to 29 and 30 points in some of the games; that's a huge amount of scoring and I suppose that's what the spectators want as well, they want to see spectacular stuff and they're certainly getting it now from the top teams.

The only downside to the modern game is you don't get to see much man-to-man contests to win the ball. In my day you stuck rigidly to your position. If you were wing back or corner-back, that's where you played. And you didn't wander too far from there. It wasn't that you stuck rigidly to your own man, but you stuck rigidly to that space and whoever came into that space. Then you had to take him and win the ball. It was zonal hurling which has come into Gaelic football recently.

The backs job was to keep the score down and get the ball down to the forwards.

The big thing we were told was to hit the ball in quickly to the forwards, so that meant we hadn't much time to look around and see who we could play it to or we'd be hooked or blocked.

The big thing you weren't to do was to blaze the ball wide. If you hit it down to the forwards with them having no chance of getting it, you were in trouble. Séan McLoughlin would let you know fairly quickly; he'd be growling at you.

Forwards in my day would have been fussy.

They would be saying to you to let it in as low as you could. The thing about keeping it low is if you're hitting it from the half-back line, it has to pass centerfield and the opposition half-backs.

If you keep it low through those two lines, there's a greater chance of being blocked and stopped. So, you have to elevate it a certain amount to get it into the inside forwards.

WE DIDN'T THINK as much about the game back then as they do now. It is really dissected now with the help of all the backroom teams and statisticians.

They are able to pinpoint what should be done and what could be done.

I think it's good; it's just the modern way.

People look into everything deeply nowadays, no matter what they are at. Everything has changed, every facet of life has changed.

My worry is that too much pre-planning is taking the instinct out of the game, as hurling is an instinctive game. With all the plans you have in your head, and all the instructions you have from the sideline before you go out, you must never forget… you're still on your own when you cross the white line. And you have to make up your mind about a lot of things, when to go and when not to go to the ball?

How you are going to clear the ball?

Where are you going to clear it to?

It's all instinctive, and the ball can change direction in an instant, getting a deflection, or if it spins off the ground or something like that, you know, you can be caught out. You can't adjudicate for everything that's going to happen and that's the beauty of hurling. It must be instinctive; you must be able to read it quicker than your opponent.

If a lad at the other end of the field hits the ball and mis-hits it a little bit, you can know when the ball hits the ground it is going to spin, one way or the other. If you're reading the game properly, you will see that, and you will know what's coming.

All that sort of stuff is instinctive, and I think that's the real beauty of the game, the lads that can read it properly like that are the lads concentrating one hundred percent all the time. That's a big failing in a lot players, especially club players nowadays, they're not concentrating on what's going on. If you're concentrating fully, you will have a fair idea of where the next ball is going to land and you'll be able to be gone before your opponent.

While that instinct is important, you have to be flexible when you go out on the field. From my point of view, I was a wing back and a wing back is a sort of a trouble-shooter. It's no use staying rigidly on your man and maybe holding him scoreless, and your team gets beaten. If someone is scoring on the far side, you'll have to go to your teammate and help out over there. The centre-back might be around it but it's no use if you stay out on your wing and keep your man scoreless.

You've got to be able to go.

That's why I call him or her a trouble-shooter.

The best wing back I have seen in a modern context was Tommy Walsh of Kilkenny.

He was a fall back to our generation; he would have been a hard grafter. He'd beat taller forwards to the ball and that showed he had that bit extra.

His distribution might not have been the best, but he did have great forwards to win their own ball. However, he rarely blazed one wide either; he might have hit them high up the field, but he knew he was keeping them within the range of the forwards. That type of hurling I would like, and I liked his attitude and the way he attacked the ball.

There were great wing backs in my time.

The Waterford team of 1959, they were a bit before my time. But Martin Óg Morrissey was centre-back on that team. He was a tremendous hurler and he could hit a ground ball the whole length of the field. They did a lot of ground hurling during that time and they swept the ball from one end to the other, and one side to the other.

Martin Coogan was a good wing back from Kilkenny. Cork had Con Roche at wing back, he was a very tidy hurler. Iggy Clarke of Galway was a very classy hurler at wing back. Into the 80s, you had Ger Coughlan in Offaly who was very good, a handy man again. In Galway there was Pete Finnerty and Gerry McInerney.

OUR GAME WAS good in our time.

The present-day game is good in its time now. I also have fierce admiration for today's hurlers because they have to put in an awful amount of time.

We trained twice a week. If we got to an All-Ireland final, we would train three times a week. There wouldn't be many training matches at the weekends as we'd be playing with our clubs anyway. The training wasn't that difficult compared to nowadays, which is very hard. They have to put in longer hours.

However, I don't think it will take the joy out of the game as I don't hear too many of the players complaining about it. They are used to this way and the methods they have nowadays.

You would think that maybe with so much time consumed on the game that they might not be enjoying it, but they seem to be, and the spectators seem to be enjoying it as well.

It's a smashing game nowadays, so fast and scores almost every minute.

It's hard to get up to that level, the amount of training they are doing is fierce. I don't know if you could do it and be a farmer like I was. I don't think I'd have the time to be doing that and the gym work, strength and conditioning as well. Like it's full-time.

I enjoy the new styles of hurling so long as the players are able to play it. Sometimes you'll see teams trying to emulate what other teams are doing. I don't think they are able, some of them; it's too intricate for them and that's a mistake.

You want to keep it simple first of all and then you try and improve it as you go along.

But start off simple. If you start off with too many ideas, players will become confused.

ALL THE MAJOR hurling counties are in the running for the All-Ireland in these times. There's five in Munster, and four in Leinster, with the likes of Carlow and Laois improving as well, though they need to get their fitness levels up as high as Limerick and Tipperary, who have raised the bar again. All the other counties will be doing that now and they will all be in with a chance of winning.

Years ago, there was only a couple of teams in the running every year. From that point of view, it is great to see the new teams coming into it and being competitive. I'd love to see Tipperary win all the time and we know that's not possible, but it's nice to see new teams coming in.

I'd love to see Waterford win one, and I wouldn't mind seeing Wexford winning one either.

Strangely enough, this year (2020) with the impact of the Coronavirus, we are likely to get a taste of old-style county hurling with the knockout format. I'm not over keen on the round robin format that was there in 2018 and '19 because there were too many chances for teams. There has to be an end point at some stage.

The only positive is it gives everyone a number of chances, where if they get caught out on a bad day, they can make up for it again… if they are good enough.

It's probably too much though, because it's taking from the club scene.

Unfortunately, there doesn't seem to be any answer or anyone coming up with a good idea to revitalise the club scene. I don't know how they are going to do it, but something must be done.

It is unfair on the clubs and it's hard to see how we rectify it because the county game is the window to show your wares at the top level, and that's what keeps the thing going. If the county teams are doing well and playing spectacular hurling, everyone else wants to do that as well and it spurs on the club game. But the clubs aren't getting the chance to show their wares and are being rushed into playing off championships at the back end of the year.

It's okay if you're involved but if you play one or two matches early in the year and you lose them, your chances are as good as gone. Then it's a pretty drab year.

I can't see how they're going to rectify it, because the managers of the county teams aren't going to release players once they are serious in the championship, and you can't blame them for that.

So, the club will have to start working really early in the year and get stuck in. At the same time, hurling is a game that needs good conditions and good pitches. Spectacular hurling will always be on the best pitches. You'll never see it on poor pitches or in poor weather conditions; you'll see tough hard games and good games, but you won't see spectacular games in bad conditions.

I would like to see clubs getting stronger and not going back grades for the sake of going back and maybe win some easy competition. It's getting harder now because the numbers aren't there in a lot of clubs to build a strong team.

EVERYONE GETS HAMMERED every now and then, but that doesn't mean you go down a grade. How many good senior teams are there in Tipperary at the moment?

You wouldn't be counting too many that you would say have really a good chance of winning a county final. But that doesn't mean that you cut the number of senior teams down to five or six and then have great games among those teams.

I believe county boards should be able to get in there and help clubs that are struggling and advise them; have good coaches go in and help them out, and maybe someone will show them how to run the club and keep the finances right. Things like that can build a club as once the spirit dies, it's very hard to get it back.

You could be doing something different such as a tractor run or whatever to make money that brings people together and you can build from there, but it is important to keep the belief in the club and in the players as well. Going down a grade, I wouldn't be a fan of that at all.

I know clubs struggle. We all struggle, but a small thing can spark a club to life again; one or two good players grow up and come into the club and drive on the senior team. That type of thing makes all the difference. We all have good players here and there, but the thing is to get six or eight on the one team and they'll drive a team then, and the rest of the guys will fall in behind.

We had a great club scene in the 60s. There were good teams and great games and some clubs might not have won county finals, but they played great games and were in the hunt every year. It wasn't possible to win every year.

Thurles Sarsfields were dominant for a long time; they won 11 out of 12 county finals. It was really hard to compete with that as they had some great hurlers all together, and Toomevara came with the same dominance in the 90s and 2000s.

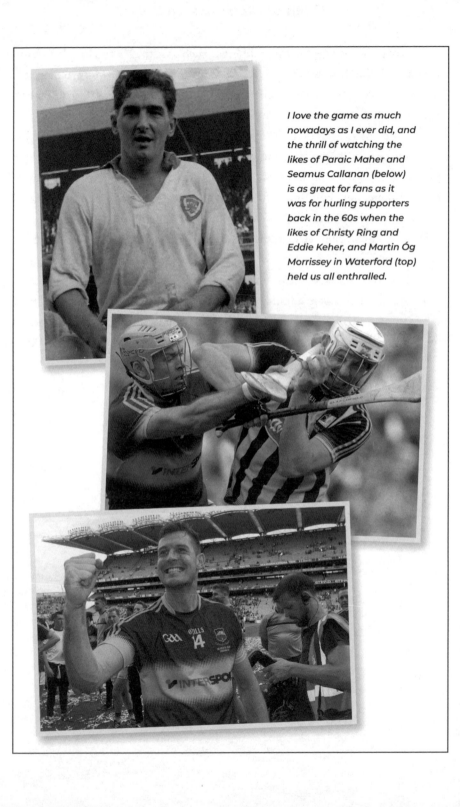

I love the game as much nowadays as I ever did, and the thrill of watching the likes of Paraic Maher and Seamus Callanan (below) is as great for fans as it was for hurling supporters back in the 60s when the likes of Christy Ring and Eddie Keher, and Martin Óg Morrissey in Waterford (top) held us all enthralled.

« CHAPTER 16 »

The Best of Company

WE ARE ALL shaped in some way by the environment we grow up in.

I was very lucky in that my parents were good, honest, decent people who worked hard and lived very productive lives. They wanted to see us do well and whatever road we took, they were behind us.

Indeed, the wider Kilruane area was always a positive community of people, and I always felt that they were wishing me well when I played on the bigger stage. On the biggest days of all, on the occasions of Munster or All-Ireland finals, I took strength from knowing they were behind me.

When Eileen and I got married in 1968, I had a decision to make as to what sort of farming I would do. Milking cows was easily the more viable option. But I felt that would be too difficult to fit in with the hurling, as cows have to be milked every day – and there were no relief milkers at that time. So, I went for tillage, sheep and beef.

This I could manage with the hurling, and my day job as an AI man.

At the time of our marriage, the 'marriage bar' was in, meaning that Eileen had to give up her job in the Civil Service. She took on the role of housewife and mother with gusto. She is renowned for her baking and cooking, and we hosted many hurling visitors down through the years. She has a speciality in making pavlova, Black Forest gateaux, and Viennese buns with jam and cream. I have a very sweet tooth, and nothing makes me happier than tucking into cake and buns, so I am a lucky man to have such a good cook!

Then, the children started coming.

AFTER OUR GREAT loss with Patrick, we thought it might never happen but in 1970 Eamonn was born safe and sound. He was the image of Patrick. We were so thrilled and thankful. All our prayers were answered.

When Fionnuala arrived the day after the 1971 All-Ireland final, it was a perfect weekend – an All-Ireland medal and a beautiful daughter. I gave her the All-Ireland medal on the day she was married.

We were so happy to have lovely, healthy children and we finished up with seven altogether. Brian was born next, then Lennie Eimear, Ciara and Sinéad. At bedtime, when we were saying the prayers with them, we would always give the children a turn to include their own intentions. This always included Patrick, deceased neighbours and hurlers. Even the great Christy Ring would get a mention.

THE FARM WAS a playground.

Health and safety was not too high on the agenda back then. The kids used to play 'Cowboys and Indians' on the straw bales in the shed… thinking they were John Wayne in the Westerns on TV.

Sheep farming had begun to decline around the area back in the 1980s and, on one occasion, while the kids were attending Kilruane NS a 'school tour' was arranged and all of the children from the school walked over to see the new-born lambs, and to feed the pet lambs with a bottle. Those were lovely innocent times.

I bought some more land about two miles away. We would walk the ewes and lambs over there in the spring. All of the kids who could walk would come. They had great fun keeping the sheep from breaking into gaps and entrances along the way. It was also a great way to help me.

I was always keen on game-shooting. The boys soon followed me and Lennie shot his first cock pheasant at 11 years of age. Both Eamonn and Lennie became crackshots and definitely had the distinction of being better than their father.

I gave them all – boys and girls – lessons on driving the tractor. At first, sitting on my lap, and then when they got bigger, taking full control. I wanted them to have a feel for it, and learn to be careful. I also wanted to do this as I had a bad experience when I was 20 – I had a Fordson Dexta tractor and the battery was run down on it so I used to have to jump-start it to get it going.

I had the technique perfected, using the gentle slope in the yard and I would give the tractor a push, and quickly jump up on it, and get it started as it was rolling.

Well, one day my plan backfired spectacularly.

I tripped as I went to jump up on the tractor and the back wheel rolled over my legs, and up along my chest. I was lucky not to be killed, and much to the doctor's surprise I didn't break a bone.

I USED TO have great fun pucking around in the yard with the kids.

They were all interested in hurling and they used to love going to training and to matches with me, meeting people from all over. It used to lighten it for me as well, when I was managing clubs or county teams – there was nothing that could not be solved over an ice cream after a match.

Eamonn hurled junior with me towards the end of my playing days. One year, he was centre-forward and I was full-forward, and we were hurling poorly against Moneygall in Nenagh. Eamonn was strong as a horse. The full-back was giving me a few digs, and didn't Eamonn see what was happening.

And he came in and stood beside me, and looked at my opponent.

'Are you alright there, dad?'

I was raging… if only he had left the 'dad' bit out.

The 'dad' part finished me… it was time to hang up the boots.

After all my years, I finally had someone to mind me.

Years later, Eamonn was asked what it was like having the distinction of having hurled with me? He swiftly replied that I had the distinction of hurling with him!

THE CHILDREN ALL have a fierce independent streak.

They all went out and found their own way in life, and Eileen and myself did not need to offer too much counsel. After college, Fionnuala hopped on her bike and cycled around Ireland. She was never short of a bed, staying with many of the families we had befriended through the game.

Growing up, Eimear was a talented musician and could turn her hand to playing the piano or the guitar, and she can sing a song. We were lucky to have a great local teacher in Eileen O'Brien Minogue, daughter of the late great Irish music maestro, Paddy O'Brien. Eimear was also a great corner-back at the camogie, and never shied away from a tackle.

Along with Ciara, Sinéad played camogie for Kilruane MacDonaghs and for St Mary's Secondary School. She travelled a lot during her Third Level studies. During her time working in Dublin, she took up Touch Rugby and went on to represent Ireland in the European Touch Rugby Championship.

FIONNUALA WAS THE first to get married, and I was an extremely proud father to walk her down the aisle to marry Eamonn Devaney. Since then, all of the children have got married.

Eamonn to Olivia Hogan.

Brian to Deirdre Cleary.

Lennie to Majella Maxwell.

Eimear to Liam Cahill.

Ciara to Jeremy Cairns.

And Sinéad to Richard Springer.

We now use any excuse to get together. With the exception of Eimear in Ballingarry, all of the children live within a 10-mile radius of our home. Luckily for me, Eileen passed on her baking skills to the girls, so there is always a great spread put out for birthdays, Communions and Confirmations.

When Sinéad married Richard, a South African native, she asked our good family friend, Bishop Willie Walsh to officiate at their wedding in Galway. One of my abiding memories from the weekend is of the South African guests mastering the art of hurling in a short space of time on the beach the next day. It appeared that their cricket skills came in useful and gave them the hand-eye co-ordination needed to get to grips with the game.

Since then, Richard's mother, Clodagh has come to live in Ireland, and is very much part of the family now.

WE ARE PROUD of our children and how they have developed. They put their families first and are very strong in the community when needed.

Lennie, a fine builder and farmer, is chairman of the local Community Alert and, like Brian, he also coaches juveniles in Kilruane MacDonaghs. Eamonn has a passion for tillage and agricultural machinery, and I often help him out where I can.

Eileen and I have 18 grandchildren and get such a kick out of seeing them growing up. We get to see so many of them daily, with them all living so close by. They range in age from three to 14, so it can get noisy, but we wouldn't have it any other way.

Luckily, our family is tight-knit and the cousins are growing up together and learning from one another. Hurling features heavily in all of their lives and there is always a match in the yard or a game of tag when they gather. We really enjoy these gatherings.

Eileen and I are back where we started, just the two of us, but surrounded by extended family and so many good neighbours and friends.

We both love dancing and the many dinner dances and medal presentations we attended over the years allowed us the opportunity to dance. Although hurling appeared to be a big part in my life, it is family that gets you through the hard days.

And family is where it begins and ends.

*Len and Eileen enjoy a
Mediterranean cruise in 2008.*

« EPILOGUE »

I GOT UNBELIEVABLE enjoyment out of hurling, right from day one.

When you're finished playing and look at the players coming on behind you, you know you were part of that at one time and were able to do it. The fact you were able to do it provides a great sense of satisfaction.

That's not being big-headed or anything, it's just a fact.

Hurling is the best game in the world.

How players play, and how they master the ball.

Control and mastery over the ball is what I call it, when you get the ball to do what you want it to do, rather than the other way around.

When you master all those things and put them together, and have a bit of grit and determination… you're the complete package. That's all needed in order to play the game. If you are in any way soft at all, you are going to stand back.

You'll be no use then.

You have to match your opponent in every way, physically, mentally and skill-wise, the whole lot. There's no way you can beat anyone on skill alone without having that drive in you to do it.

It takes the lot.

Hurling is limitless.

You can really hit the heights if you can get your body and your mind in order. I used to see Jimmy Doyle doing things in training and if someone hit him a pass, he'd say to hit it harder… 'I'll catch it, don't worry,' he'd say.

He was able to do it and would control a ball under your nose if it came hard enough at him. He was so quick to react. Those kind of men have that bit extra. The rest of us might not be as good as them, but they bring us on.

IF I COULD do it all over again, I'd do it twice as hard as I loved every minute of it. I got great satisfaction out of hurling. It was always there. Other things might go wrong, or you might not be happy about something or other, but hurling was always there for me either as a player, coach, or father.

It took my mind off everything for whatever length of time.

There hasn't been a day that I don't think about hurling and having no hurling because of the Coronavirus nearly killed me. I missed it that much.

When I was younger, I often went down to the ball alley on Christmas Day and I'd hurl my way down there and on the way back. I always found the hurley as a sort of a companion really.

I was comfortable in my own company and once I had a hurley, a ball and a wall I was happy.

I never just hit the ball off the wall. I was hitting it with purpose every time, to try to get it to come back to me a certain way or to try to do something different.

I asked Tony Wall one time, after losing a match, is there anything I can do better and he said, 'If you could practice on grass with a sliotar it would be better'.

Rapla House was a ruin nearby and it had a large rough gable end wall with one small window at the top. I could belt away there without causing any damage and I tried that, and I got great satisfaction out of it.

If it were only a straight wall and was coming back straight all the time, I wouldn't get that much satisfaction out of it. I loved to have the ball coming back differently to keep me on my toes.

I hurled because I loved doing it.

I wasn't trying to make myself better to get on the Tipp team or the Kilruane team, I just loved playing.

I don't know why I had such a strong feeling for hurling.

But I had.

And still have to this day.

« ON LEN »

MICHAEL BABS KEATING

HE WAS THE most enthusiastic and committed of Tipperary hurlers, and has remained committed ever since. The hours and the days and the weeks and the months that Len put into the GAA was incredible.

As a colleague there was none better.

Len joined the minor ranks with me and then through under-21 and senior, and with him and Eileen we had a great relationship with my wife, Nancy and myself.

Len got married 10 days before me in 1968. He was at my wedding, but I wasn't able to go to his wedding as I was on my honeymoon. We had a lot of similarities down through the years.

When I lived in Nenagh from 1973 to '77 I was a regular visitor to Len's house.

MACKEY MCKENNA

HE WAS STONE mad about hurling.

He could talk about hurling as well. I'd often ask him about the lad I would be marking, and he'd say, 'Mackey… you'll handle him alright'.

He'd never say do this or do that; he'd say, 'You can handle him'.

EDDIE KEHER

HE WAS SUCH a dedicated hurling man to the game in general, as well as to his own game.

Looking back on his career, hurling was the number one with him, whether it was playing or training teams.

The fact that he promoted hurling and became the manager of Clare, who were great Tipperary rivals, and brought them to a level where they could compete for Munster and All-Ireland titles in the 90s, was phenomenal.

PAT MCLOUGHNEY

IF YOU WERE doing laps of the field and he saw a lad struggling, he would come up to him and have a go in a nice way asking, 'Where were you last night?'… or, 'I heard something about you at the weekend.'

In his own way he was coaxing a fella along without him really knowing it. Another guy would be critical for not putting in the effort, whereas Len approached it in a different manner.

At the same time if you were messing in a training session, he would be fairly quick to let you know.

He had a great way with players.

EAMON O'SHEA

WHAT I PICKED up from him, more so than anything else, was the sense when you step on a pitch as a trainer, coach or a manager, the players take their lead from you. And if you are not on it, and you don't bring that energy and passion, the session won't be good.

I got a major share of that energy from him and from that time.

I see Liam Sheedy and I see elements of Len in him as well. Liam and I are different people and we complement one another but the one thing we do have in common is we have to have belief, and Len definitely would have made a huge contribution to that.

BISHOP WILLIE WALSH

HE DID A great job with Clare. The players had great time for him, and he had great respect for the players.

He was a great man to motivate a team but in his coaching, he was very traditional in his approach.

Len brought something special to it. He was the right man at the right time. He got the players to believe in themselves. He got them to respect the jersey again. Respect more than anything else was the key message he got across.

Once players came on board, they wanted to stay on board whereas before his arrival players were dropping out every year.

Above all, while he is a hurling man, Len Gaynor is a fine rounded individual. Hurling is very important but family, his children and grandchildren, are top of the list as far as he is concerned. Next would be community.

He is a man of great integrity and honesty. Testament to a man at 76 years of age is every Wednesday across the summer he is in the field in Ardcroney coaching kids from six to 14 years of age.

That says a lot about the man and the great promise for hurling in the parish, as the seeds are sown there for these boys and girls for their love of hurling.

Len himself has such a love for hurling he passes that on automatically.

GER LOUGHNANE

THE FIRST THING that jumps into my mind about Len Gaynor is seeing him as a player – the incredible determination he had, the toughness he had, as well as the hurling ability of course.

He wasn't as physically powerful as the rest, but he came in there with sheer grit and determination and the will to win. Not only did he hold his own, but he became one of the vital links in that team.

As a manager, he was so good at getting players to commit to the thing and give everything they had. He brightened up the training sessions with his optimism and energy.

The thing that shone out is he was such a genuine guy.

You knew he was there for the hurling only, not the publicity part of it. He just loved the teams he had playing good hurling.

We would never have been that close.

That's often the way with selectors over a team. We wouldn't have been ringing each other a lot outside of training; we'd just meet up at training where we got on great. There was great camaraderie between us.

We enjoyed each other's company and chatting about hurling, but we never got close. I have massive respect for him, not alone as a hurling man but as a person. He is so honourable, has such great integrity.

An absolutely decent person and a model person.

ANTHONY DALY

HE USED TO have a saying… 'Give it your living best'… and when he said it he meant you to give your absolute living best. It was the way he said it; you realised that he was pouring his 'living best' into that as well.

I have used that saying with teams over the years, to give everything that is inside of you. Sometimes lads don't know the meaning of that, that it's just something thrown out there by any manager.

He was very specific about what he wanted from that.

He took on our team at an awful low base. He brought us to an awful lot near its best on given days, but that ultimate belief wasn't there yet. He brought that whole sense of… 'We are in this together,' and a real purpose and I got no sense that that was there before he arrived. That's the big thing he did for us.

Even on the Monday nights after losing the Munster finals, even as a non-drinker he'd join us and make sure we didn't make a show of ourselves. He always had that touch that he was looking out for us.

Everybody in Clare would recognise the work he did.

Ger Loughnane did bring it to another level but if he had not been involved with Len for two of the four years as a selector, he wouldn't have seen the work that was going on and the potential that was there.

SÉAN FOGARTY

I'M NOT ONE bit surprised the success Len Gaynor had on the field of play, and indeed off it.

The determination he would show at county board meetings and county conventions… anything he said, his heart and soul was in it. You could feel the strength in his voice, he was so passionate about any point he wanted to make.

MURT DUGGAN

LEN WAS A serious hurling man and wanted fellas to play with a bit of fire in their belly, the way he played himself.

I would consider him a friend. I would have great regard for him.

He was always the real Len Gaynor.

MICHAEL DOYLE

THE ONE THING I would always say about Len is it's like the ad on the television for buying paint, it's exactly what you get on the tin.

Len was dead straightforward. If he had something to say he would say it and that was it. He would never say anything behind a person's face. We never fell out as a management; we had our disagreements on picking teams but that would be about it.

MICHAEL CLEARY

HE WOULD ALWAYS be held in the highest esteem hurling wise.

He was an outstanding hurler but also a good man. He was fiercely determined. He had a fierce determined walk about him; he still has that.

You always admired the way he carried himself and then as I got to know him in later years, what you would hear coming out of his mouth, you could see how the man was put together.

That's the Len I got to know playing under him with Tipperary and then bounced off a fair bit in my time as Tipperary camogie manager, as he was at all the matches with Ciara.

It wasn't foolhardy single-mindedness, it was just a single-minded focus on playing well and winning, doing the thing well and doing it right.

Doing it fiercely determined. Doing it for Tipperary or doing it for your club, yourself, your family.

I used to love that.

One Sunday, I remember going down to the old dressing-rooms at half-time in Nenagh when Kilruane were playing, just to hear what he was saying. I could hear Len talking to them and he used the expression… 'We want to play manfully, skilfully… and to the final whistle.'

It just sums up hurling.

LIAM SHEEDY

HE'S A MASSIVELY passionate hurling man. He has a fierce drive and passion for the game of hurling. Also, his whole honesty of approach and honesty of effort.

He was a real ball of energy. He was always out there leading the line, rolling up the sleeves. He wouldn't ask you to do anything he wasn't prepared to do himself.

I was only coming of age when I saw him coming on as a sub for Kilruane in the late 70s in matches in Nenagh and he was still contributing.

He had a brilliant way of connecting with people of all ages.

In the latter years I was going to schools and seeing how respected he was among the kids because of all the work he did on the coaching side. He was so giving of his time and energy to everybody as all he wanted to do was make a difference, whether you were a child in a school in Ballina or Kilruane. He was able to touch off all age groups and I think it is a unique skill to connect with people of all ages. He had that skill.

Those values and attributes that Len Gaynor has, that's what you would be happy to see in yourself; try and take leaf out of his book. The passion he had for the team and for the county, the honesty of approach, he didn't have any hidden agendas or any ego, he just wanted Tipp and the team to do well at all costs.

And he was willing to do everything he possibly could to do that.

Anytime you interact with people like that you are looking to see what made them so good and certainly I'd like to think there are aspects of his management style and the way he approached things that rubbed off on me in a positive way, and helped me in my quest to be a successful inter-county manager.

Passion was the key attribute and it is the one I look to try and bring as well.

It's not easy, but that was certainly something he had, and I would be quite happy if I was being compared to Len Gaynor in terms of passion and energy because he was superb in that regard.

LIAM CAHILL

I WOULD HAVE got an awful lot of passion from his management style as regards the standard he expected you to be when you not just played for Tipp, but played the game of hurling. He always gave me a fierce impression of how you behave as a Tipperary hurler.

He has a lot of strengths to him that way.

He liked players to man up and win their own ball.

He didn't take excuses lightly.

He wasn't a lover of people being on the physio table either, which we probably needed at the time to give us a little more hardness because there were a few lads that liked to be on the table a lot.

He took a lot of excuses away.

He is a good Tipperary man and Irish man who prides himself on the basics of what life is about. Even to this day, he is as enthusiastic as ever, and I don't think I have ever met him in bad form.

He's enthused every time he meets his grandchildren.

JOHN LEAHY

I HAVE GOOD memories of Len Gaynor being Tipperary manager. We had good times in the dressing-room with him.

We got to an All-Ireland final. Len has to take all the credit for that.

John Leahy might not have been part of all that, but for Len Gaynor. Another manager might have decided I wouldn't have been part of it but I was part of it because Len Gaynor made a decision that it would be good for John Leahy to stay playing hurling for Tipperary and it would be good for Tipperary hurling as well.

It was more than just hurling; it is a hobby I loved, and it got me through the second year of coming out of a tough time.

FATHER TOM FOGARTY

HE'S ONE OF the great GAA figures of our time.

What impressed me about him is that with the game evolving so much in his time, Len embraced the changes that took place. He never lived in the past.

He is a brilliant coach and what I liked about the man is that there is no ego in Len Gaynor whatsoever. If you asked Len Gaynor to train a junior team or an under-10 team he would. He would never look for remuneration either, it would be for the love of the game. That says a lot about a person.

Also, he has a superb value system.

He has great respect for people as well.

I found working with him that his knowledge of the game was second to none.

He is an utterly unassuming man and never talked about his own achievements on the field. He might refer to them to make a point but he never focused on what he won and all the accolades that he achieved.

BRIAN CARTHY

I ALWAYS REGARDED it as a deep privilege to work with Len on RTÉ Radio Sport. He was one of the all-time greats of hurling. As a youngster I saw quite a few championship clashes involving Tipperary.

The thing that stands out is his passion for hurling.

Another thing that is sometimes not noticed is he is a very modest man, not looking to be in the front seat and that says a lot about him as a person.

CIARA GAYNOR

IN ONE WAY he was just dad and we looked up to him in that respect. No matter who came into the house he was always talking hurling.

Everything was hurling.

You'd get introduced as Len Gaynor's child so you knew he was respected in hurling circles, but we wouldn't have known to what extent.

He was so passionate about it.

When Covid-19 struck, he wasn't worried about getting sick. His first comment was, 'What am I going to do without the hurling?'

He lives for it.

LEN GAYNOR
ROLL OF HONOUR

PLAYER

TIPPERARY

3 – All Ireland Senior Hurling Championship (1964, '65, '71)

5 – Munster Senior Hurling Championship (1964, '65, '67, '68 '71)

2 – National Hurling League (1965, '68)

4 – Oireachtas Cup (1964, '65, '68, '70)

3 – Railway Cup (1968, '69, '70)

1 – Cú Chulainn Award (pre-All Stars) (1968)

1 – All Ireland Under-21 Hurling Championship (1964)

2 – Munster Under-21 Hurling Championship (1964, '65)

1 – Munster Minor Hurling Championship (1962)

KILRUANE MACDONAGHS

3 – Tipperary Senior Hurling Championship (1977, '78, '79)

4 – North Tipperary Senior Hurling Championship (1965, '77, '78, '79)

1 – Tipperary Junior Hurling Championship (1985)

1 – North Tipperary Junior Hurling Championship (1985)

1 – Tipperary Under-15 Hurling Championship (1959)

1 – North Tipperary Under-15 Hurling Championship (1959)

ST FLANNAN'S

1 – Dean Ryan Cup (1961)

[continued]

LEN GAYNOR
ROLL OF HONOUR

MANAGEMENT

4 years as Clare Senior Hurling manager (1991-94)

2 years as Tipperary Senior Hurling manager (1997-98)

2 years as Tipperary Intermediate Hurling manager (2005-06)

4 years as Tipperary Senior Hurling selector (1983-86)

7 years as Tipperary Under-21 Hurling selector (1974-77, 2005-07)

2 years as Tipperary Minor Hurling selector (1972-73)

13 years as Kilruane MacDonaghs Senior Hurling coach (1977-89)

1 – All Ireland Club Hurling Championship (Kilruane MacDonaghs 1986)

2 – Munster Club Hurling Championship
(Moycarkey Borris, 1982; Kilruane MacDonaghs 1985)

6 – Tipperary Senior County Hurling Championship
(Kilruane MacDonaghs 1977, '78, '79, '85; Moycarkey Borris 1982;
Clonoulty Rossmore 1989)

6 – North Tipperary Senior Hurling Championship
(Kilruane MacDonaghs 1977, '78, '79, '85, '86, '87)

2 – Tipperary Intermediate Club Hurling Championship
(Shannon Rovers 1986, Newport 1989)

2 – North Tipperary Intermediate Club Hurling Championship
(Shannon Rovers 1986, Newport 1989)

5 – Tipperary Under-21 Hurling Championship
(**4** with Kilruane MacDonaghs, **1** with Moneygall)

5 – North Tipperary Under-21 Hurling Championship
(**4** with Kilruane MacDonaghs and **1** with Moneygall)

1 – Tipperary Minor Hurling Championship (Kilruane MacDonaghs 1971)

3 – North Tipperary Minor Hurling Championship
(Kilruane MacDonaghs 1971, '72, '73)

Nenagh Guardian **Hall of Fame Award 2017**

MORE
GREAT
SPORTS BOOKS
FROM
HEROBOOKS

www.**HERO**BOOKS.digital

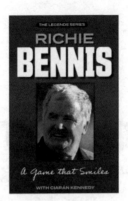

'A Game that Smiles'
The Richie Bennis Autobiography

RICHIE BENNIS IS one of the true legends remaining in the game of hurling. A towering figure in Limerick GAA, he played a central role as the county won the All-Ireland title in 1973 and then he strived as hard as anyone to see the Liam MacCarthy Cup return to the Treaty County.

It was a wait of 45 years – during which time Bennis worked at grassroots hurling in the famed Patrickswell club, where he hurled into his 40s and won 10 county titles. He also led Limerick as team manager to the 2007 All-Ireland final where they lost to Kilkenny.

In 2018, Limerick were crowned All-Ireland champions.

For Richie Bennis, a long agonising wait ended. His story is one of triumph, and heartache and personal tragedy, and a courage that was never dimmed.

Authors: Richie Bennis with Ciarán Kennedy
Print Price: €20.00
ISBN: 9781910827093

Available on
Amazon
Apple Books
Kobo
And all good book shops

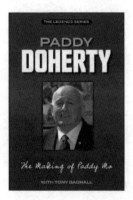

The Making of Paddy Mo
Paddy Doherty: An Autobiography

TO THIS DAY, Down's Paddy Doherty is still remembered as one of the most lethal finishers in the history of Gaelic football. The Ballykinlar clubman was fast, and breathtaking on the ball.

He led his county to a long awaited All-Ireland victory in 1960, and the following summer he captained the Mournemen and brought the Sam Maguire Cup back across the border a second time.

Doherty continued to rip apart defences throughout the decade and won a third All-Ireland crown with Down in 1968, when the Mournemen defeated Kerry in September for the second time, to add to seven Ulster titles and three National league titles.

The 1960s was a decade which is best remembered for the legend of Paddy Doherty.

And... The Making of Paddy Mo.

Authors: Paddy Doherty with Tony Bagnall
Print Price: €20.00
Ebook: €10.00
ISBN: 9781910827178

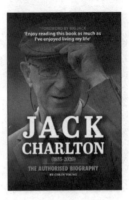

Jack Charlton
The Authorised Biography

AS ONE OF the true legends of Irish and English football, Jack Charlton was a man both loved and feared, but now the people who have lived with him all of his life introduce the real 'Big Jack' in this brilliant authorised biography which is presented in a foreword by Jack himself.

For the first time Jack's wife and family, his teammates as a World Cup winner with England in 1966, and his players during his management years with Middlesbrough, Sheffield Wednesday, Newcastle, and Ireland tell their stories of the man who dominated their lives.

Graeme Souness, Chris Waddle, and Peter Beardsley amongst others, are joined by Mick McCarthy, Niall Quinn and the greatest footballers who played under Big Jack for 10 years as Ireland team boss.

This is the most personable, inviting and intimate account of Jack Charlton's life, and the book contains photographs published for the first time from Jack and Pat Charlton's personal collection.

Jack Charlton: The Authorised Biography is written by former Daily Mail Northern Football Correspondent, Colin Young.

Author: Colin Young
Print Price: €20.00
Ebook: €10.00
ISBN: 9781910827017

Available on
Amazon

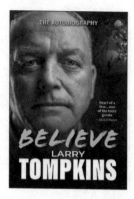

BELIEVE

Larry Tompkins: An Autobiography

HIS SELF-BELIEF WAS unbreakable.

His iron will inspirational.

Nothing could stop Larry Tompkins. No man, no team, as he made his football life the greatest story ever told in the long and brilliant history of the GAA.

Six years with his native Kildare left him empty-handed and heartbroken. He emigrated to New York to find a job and find a team he could lead to championship glory. In the United States, Tompkins' belief in himself never dimmed. He led Donegal to four New York championships in the Big Apple. He also found a new home for himself in Ireland and led Castlehaven to two Cork and Munster titles. In between, he also became the most valuable and feared footballer in Ireland.

BELIEVE is the story of a man who defied all the odds. In Cork's magnificent red shirt, he led his adopted county to two All-Ireland titles in 1989 and 90, one National League and six Munster titles, and he also was honoured with three Allstar awards.

Upon his retirement, Larry Tompkins continued to lead and inspire, and make others believe too. He managed Cork for seven years, winning Munster glory again, and drove Cork to the 1999 All-Ireland final where they agonisingly came up short.

BELIEVE is a story which proves to everyone, in every sport, that anything is possible and everything is there to be won!

Authors: Larry Tompkins with Denis Hurley
Print Price: €20.00
Ebook: €10.00
ISBN: 9781910827123

Available on
Amazon
Apple Books
Kobo
And all good online stores

TIPPERARY
GAME OF MY LIFE

THE GREATEST TIPPERARY hurlers over the last 50 years remember the one game in blue and gold that defined their lives...

Jimmy Finn, Theo English, Tony Wall, Tadhg O'Connor, Dinny Ryan, Babs Keating, John Sheedy, Ken Hogan, Colm Bonnar, Cormac Bonnar, Declan Carr, Michael Cleary, Pat Fox, Conal Bonnar, Declan Ryan, Michael Ryan, Joe Hayes, Eamonn Corcoran, Tommy Dunne, Shane McGrath, James Woodlock, Brendan Cummins, Eoin Kelly, Michael Cahill, Brendan Maher, James Barry, Seamus Callinan and more...

A game that will live with each man forever.

Author: Stephen Gleeson
Print Price: €20.00
Ebook: €10.00
ISBN: 9781910827185

Available on
Amazon
Apple Books
Kobo
And all good online stores